DIRECT YOUR SUBCONSCIOUS
and drive to success

DIRECT YOUR SUBCONSCIOUS
and drive to success

Paul Harris

foulsham

LONDON • NEW YORK • TORONTO • SYDNEY

foulsham

Yeovil Road, Slough, Berkshire SL1 4JH

ISBN 0-572-01573-9

Printed in Great Britain at St Edmundsbury Press, Bury St Edmunds

CONTENTS

I dedicate this book to a very special young lady without whose enthusiasm, inspiration and patience (which, fortunately, outweigh her inability to spell) this book, its message and hopefully your subsequent success, would not have been possible. Thanks Al.

P. R. W. Harris

FOREWORD

The method outlined in this book can be applied to almost any situation where a high level of concentration, willpower and determination is required. Although this technique is extremely effective when used to attain a specific goal in a *direct* manner, it may also be used to overcome certain problems by tackling them in an *indirect* manner. By this, I mean that certain problems, bad habits, phobias, etc., are surmountable or avoidable if the appropriate qualities of personality and character have been developed.

At the end of this section I have listed a few of the areas to which this book, and the procedures detailed within it, may be applied. As you read through the list you will probably realise additional applications, relating to your own personal desires, ambitions or problems.

The potential of the technique that I will show you is vast. Once you understand *how* and *why* it works and have been familiarised with the procedures involved, you will be able to apply it to any area of your life to bring swift successful results. For the sake of simplicity, the examples that I have used in the following pages have been designed with the *direct* method of goal fulfilment in mind. The procedures, however, are identical for achieving the intangible goals that I refer to, and the traits of personality and character required to overcome certain inadequacies (i.e. the ability to concentrate, confidence, self-discipline, the ability to relax, courage, etc.).

Whether your personal desire be success in a particular sport, promotion at work, performing arts, etc., or success in overcoming a phobia or addiction, or attaining certain personality factors, or simply self-improvement, then *Direct Your Subconscious and Drive to Success* contains the answers, the procedures and the techniques necessary for attaining all of your goals.

APPLICATIONS

Competitive sports.
Performing Arts. (Acting, singing, dancing, music).
Business. (Reaching the top in your chosen
profession/starting your own company).
Overcoming a speech impediment.
Overcoming bad memory.
Slimming.
Avoiding, or aiding the recovery from, depression.
Modelling.
Overcoming day to day problems and frustration.
Overcoming a drink problem. (Aid not cure).
Reducing or eliminating stress.
Meeting the opposite sex. (Shyness).
Insomnia. (Sleep disorders).
Improving interview techniques.
Apathy (General lack of interest in life).
Sex (Overcome problems relating to your sexual
behaviour).
Lack of confidence.
Phobias. (Heights, open spaces, closed spaces,
spiders, snakes etc.).
Smoking. (An aid to giving it up).
Preparing yourself for examinations.
Fears (Dentist, doctor – pain etc.).
Nervous fidgeting.
Nail biting.
General self-improvement.

I am sure that you can, and will, find many more
applications for the contents of this book, thus
improving your life and realising all of your
ambitions.

CHAPTER ONE

THE FIRST STEP

You have now taken the first step towards achieving any degree of success that you truly desire. No matter whether your personal interest is business, sport, performing arts, or simply self-improvement, the procedures I have outlined in the following pages will work for you! The only prerequisites are desire and belief, which will be discussed later.

Having led you through the following pages, I know you will possess the knowledge to enable you to succeed in every aspect of your life, if that is your wish.

Well, let us pause for a moment. Re-reading the above sentence you will probably realise that this is a promise without limitations. I would hazard a guess that you have already begun to restrict what this book can actually teach you. Your habit-conditioned mind has rejected the possibility of truth in this statement.

If you are wise you will cast aside failure-oriented doubt and deadly self-limitation long enough to learn how I propose to fulfil my promise.

I would not expect you to accept my statement without evidence. But you must accept the possibility that *Direct Your Subconscious and Drive to Success* just might work for you. The fact is that the principles you are to receive have worked, without exception, for everyone who has tried them. In the process of my research I have uncovered numerous spectacular success stories. However, the true extent of its success is uncertain. As is always the secret with power, those who are fortunate enough to have gained it, are in no great hurry to broadcast the formula. They would rather keep the powerful advantage that they have received to themselves.

The discovery of these simple but astonishingly effective natural laws goes back as far as the 1950s, when key executives of highly successful American corporations became aware of the power of what I call Subconscious Reprogramming Technique.

Soon a number of very expensive but extremely successful seminars and private sessions were being carried out by various practitioners. Although the price for these services was high (thousands of dollars!) it seemed insignificant beside the incredible success stories which resulted from the application of the secrets they had learned. To ensure the secrecy of this new discovery, only a selective group of elite people were even informed of the opportunity to attend one of these power-sessions. The subscription fees were so high that attendance was limited still further. The desire for secrecy was so great that the closed meetings were all held away from civilisation in desert and mountain retreats.

Research into reprogramming continued and, from the results, certain patterns began to emerge. These patterns explained why some people achieve great success while others remain in obscurity. From this, certain guidelines and rules became apparent, which could eliminate failure for those who followed them. If you can learn how to apply

11

reprogramming to your life, you will never again look at a particularly successful person and think 'I wish I were as lucky as he is'. You will know that 'luck' and 'fate' are not significant factors in success or failure; 'luck' is, in fact, a direct result of the correct application of natural laws, which anyone can tap into and use to effect their success.

This power is comparable to any one of the natural energy sources (electricity, gas, wind etc.). It does not have to be created; it already exists in nature. A method must be discovered, however, to 'plug in' and utilise this force for our own benefit.

The discovery is restricted at first until its true potential has been established, but eventually it is available for everyone to apply to their individual requirements. It is also true that every one of these powers must be correctly handled for beneficial use. If mistreated they can become destructive and work against you.

It will probably become apparent as you study this book and learn about reprogramming, that your failures have been caused by your own misuse of powers that you weren't even aware of. You will learn why you have not been more successful than you have, and more importantly how to rectify that situation.

You are now on your way to undoing past mistakes and creating a dynamic, successful new lifestyle. It is imperative however that you are aware of exactly *what* you want out of life. You should cover every aspect you feel is important to success, whether this is work, health, possessions, excitement, or pastime. Everybody's view will be slightly different.

Part of the work ahead involves detailing an exact answer to the question of what you actually desire. Surveys have shown that people who create effective plans for achieving their desires stand a better chance of achieving their goals and fulfilling their lives. No truly successful person has attained success without a specific plan. A wise man once explained that there were really only three kinds of failure:

(i) The man who has well-defined goals, who knows exactly where he wants to go, but never quite gets there. His failings are due to the ineffective pursuit of his goals. He is unable to overcome his drawbacks by using effectively whatever assets he possesses.

(ii) The man who has the desire to succeed, he pushes hard making use of every asset, but fails because he has no well-defined goals. This man is like a powerful ship... with no rudder. He always seems to be making great headway but never arrives.

(iii) This man is doomed to failure, he has neither well-defined goals nor is he effective. It could be said that his ship has no rudder and no engine.

Do any of these seem a little too familiar? If you are honest you will probably agree, that your shortcomings in the past were the result of your attempt falling into one of these three categories. Well, that is definitely a thing of the past. From here on, dramatic changes will start taking place in your life.

Through the consistent use of reprogramming you will find yourself in a position to select specific goals and achieve the effectiveness that will allow you to reach them.

Intelligence, enthusiasm, good health, luck etc. are assets to be used effectively, but they do not determine success or failure. Thousands of people who started out with supposedly severe handicaps, such as ill health, shyness and bad luck have become pre-eminently successful. The method of reprogramming laid down in the following pages is neither complicated nor time-consuming. However, the technique is extremely powerful, and is, I feel, the single most effective and speedy route to success. It is the key, which, if used correctly, will enable you to fulfil your ambitions and attain all of your goals.

THE LEARNING PROCESS

It is important that you do not just *read* this book, you must also *perform*, in order to reap all of the benefits offered by subconscious reprogramming. To understand fully and learn the principles of reprogramming, I would suggest that, as you read on, you use the following guidelines to enhance your ability to absorb the information that I offer.

(i) READ the book completely and either underline or highlight any key phrases or principles. It may be helpful to keep a notebook handy in which to record brief notes and comments.

Alternatively, having thoroughly read through the book, underlining and highlighting as you go, return to the beginning and page through, using the key phrases to record a concise summary in your note book. I have found this technique to be very useful, as it would seem that by simply *re-writing* an important comment it is immediately committed to memory.

If you do no more than simply read through the following pages you cannot really expect to *learn* anything, and although it may be interesting reading, you will have missed your opportunity to benefit from its contents, and through the understanding of this, realise your true potential.

(ii) STUDY as you read. Take time to stop and think about what is being said. You must do more than merely apply your eyes to the printed page, you must also apply your mind. To understand anything other than the simplest of things, one must study.

To benefit from reprogramming it is necessary to understand *how* and *why* it works. Having reached this stage, you must then understand *how* to utilise its power and successfully apply it to your individual requirement.

(iii) PERFORM the simple steps that I have outlined, in great detail, in the chapters which lie ahead. You must actually try the techniques that I have described. It is only from trial and then dedicated practice, that you will master these techniques. It is only through continued use of these techniques that you will learn how stimulating and effective the process of reprogramming can be.

The power of reprogramming has been scientifically studied and researched resulting in certain techniques, the use of which will guarantee success. All that is required now, is for you to implement these techniques.

CHAPTER TWO

TOO PROUD TO RUN?

At this point I would like to say just a few words to the sceptics amongst you. During your study of reprogramming and the learning process you are about to undertake, there will undoubtedly be a few grumblings and mutterings of 'mumbo-jumbo', 'it couldn't be that straightforward' or words to that effect. Well it *is* straightforward, and if you do not give it your undying attention, and actually *TRY* the techniques I have outlined, you will have deprived yourself of the opportunity to attain that elusive success.

All that is required from you is a little time and, if not belief, then at least an open mind. And I am sure that you will agree, this is a very small price to pay, when you consider the incredible results that can be and have been achieved through the correct application of reprogramming techniques.

You obviously possess a burning desire for success; after all you purchased this book. That decision could very well change the rest of your life. Once again the choice is yours. Don't let sceptical obstinacy cloud your mind, or it will be your downfall. Understand that you have *nothing* to lose, and perhaps *everything* to gain – with such overwhelming odds, surely you must at least try.

'Don't miss the boat because you are too proud to run!'

Remember this. Apply its principle to your life at the appropriate points of decision, and you will have no regrets.

Now, you may be wondering why I am trying so hard to convince you. Well, it's simple: I have made you a promise and I want to keep it. I know the effect that reprogramming can have on an individual's life – *could* have on *your* life. I have uncovered incredible success stories, resulting from the correct application of reprogramming, but I can only offer you the techniques. The practice and eventual perfection of these techniques is up to you. In an attempt to convince you still further, let me show you how I stumbled across reprogramming, and it reformed my whole lifestyle.

Back in the 1970s I was regularly practising the oriental art of Judo. I progressed well initially, attaining a certain degree of success in gradings and at championships. However, I reached a point where my achievements seemed to 'level off '. I increased my training programme and began lifting weights to accelerate my rate of progress. As a result of this I continued to improve, until once again the reward for my efforts diminished. It was at this point that I began using, in a very crude form, what I now know to be subconscious reprogramming techniques. This basically took two forms: the definition of my goals and then the visualisation. My practice of these techniques followed no logical pattern and was by no means consistent. But the results were devastating. Within three months I became the North West Champion, and regularly placed in the top three at Regional Championships. My success continued until I eventually earned a position at the National Selections for the British Judo Squad. Shortly after this I discovered a series of articles in a bodybuilding magazine, relating to self-hypnosis. The technique described was that of reprogramming, and was fundamentally what I had been practising over the past months. I immediately began to apply these refined techniques to my workouts in the gym, and once again, the results I received were astonishing. My poundages rose sharply and my ability to concentrate increased, allowing my workouts to become intense and highly effective. Within the first four weeks my body weight was up seven pounds and, in certain instances, poundages had increased fifty percent.

Since those early days I have applied reprogramming techniques to several aspects of my life, surmounting my inadequacies, building and strengthening personal qualities to re-sculpture my self-image, progressing at work and most recently founding my own company, the success of which is attributable to the enthusiastic practice of reprogramming.

Incidentally, my training partner recently returned to the Judo mat after a 'lay-off' of approximately five years. He now boasts a position on the British Judo Squad after winning a gold medal at the National Selections, after a training period of only seven months. Needless to say, during this period, he supplemented his rigorous training schedule with daily sessions of reprogramming.

As I have already explained, the benefits of reprogramming are not restricted to sports; they can be applied to any aspect of one's life. Remember the key executives of successful American organisations back in the 1950s and their secret meetings? Well, the very same principles that they were learning are being used in business today, reportedly earning one man $17,000 in a day, and another averaging $19,000 a month, and yet another who returned from a $50,000 debt to own several successful businesses, is earning $200,000 a year. Then there is the man who said he'd had a stuttering problem most of his life, and had cured it in three days using what we call subconscious reprogramming techniques. Convinced yet? Well hopefully I have aroused enough interest in even the most sceptical of you, to enable you to proceed uninhibited through the following pages with an open mind.

I am not asking you to 'believe it'. I am asking you to 'try it' and judge for yourself.

Using the material in this book, you could have everything you really want from life. The only thing that may prevent you, is your existing inadequate self-image.

It may be difficult to shake loose from the negative forces that govern your present life, because you have become accustomed to them. They have grown up with you and, in the passage of time, become accepted.

However your destiny lies in your own hands. By the correct application of reprogramming techniques you can change.

CHAPTER THREE

FAILING TO SUCCEED

Success can be intimidating and even threatening to those who feel that they do not deserve it. It is for this reason that many people whom you see at work, in the gym, on the television etc. progress rapidly towards the top, then, just as everyone expects them to break through to even greater success, they begin to slide downhill.

I believe that the reason for this is due largely to the fact that if you feel that you really don't deserve success, then your subconscious will form a mental barrier and you will reject and resist any form of recognition.

To free yourself from these destructive negative thoughts, you must change your attitudes and expectations concerning who you are, and what degree of success you feel that you are entitled to.

This is done by establishing a new unrestricted self-image in your subconscious, perceiving your potential differently than you do now. The process of changing an undeserving or fearful attitude towards success can be directly related to the process of motivation towards a goal. As a new idea, (perhaps a desirable personal quality such as efficiency, energy or concentration) is implanted in the subconscious and consistently reinforced, then it becomes comfortable and acceptable. With dedicated practice and reinforcement, your expectations gradually move in a new direction, until you finally rise above any self-imposed limitations. Remember, the only limitations that exist are those that we acknowledge.

I would point out that these limitations are not intentional; they are unconscious reactions stemming from the person's belief that he or she is either inadequate or unworthy of success. This may be the result of a past failure in a similar area or because parental influence did not build that person's confidence sufficiently in childhood.

In view of this, it becomes clear that the only way to overcome these mental restrictions is by convincing the subconscious mind that you are a successful and highly effective person or at least have the ability to be so.

It is at the point where your subconscious has accepted this, that you actually become all of those things, you feel comfortable with success, and success comes easily. Once you have accepted your potential, people around you will notice your increased confidence and will begin to treat you differently. Your advice will be sought. This will obviously bring further self-assurance and you will soon realise how true is the saying that 'success breeds success'.

It is simply a matter of replacing false beliefs that you have, through repetition, with positive and unwavering belief in your ability to be successful. By following this simple rule, you can achieve any degree of success that you truly desire.

The fundamental law of cause and effect is at work here. Your present state, perhaps anxiety, inhibition or self-sabotage is the 'effect' that you are experiencing, the 'cause' being your inadequate self-image. If you can change this 'cause' using the techniques that I have outlined, then the 'effect' will also change, leaving you able to progress, unrestricted, to your true potential.

Your subconscious mind will serve you in the way in which it has been programmed. It will, through neglect or indifference, be programmed by circumstance or chance. By reprogramming you may remove, alter or amend old thought patterns and beliefs with positive suggestions.

INADEQUATE SELF-IMAGE

Almost everyone suffers from an inadequate self-image, some obviously to a greater extent than others. There is a direct relationship between your self-image and the ability to succeed. This is illustrated below.

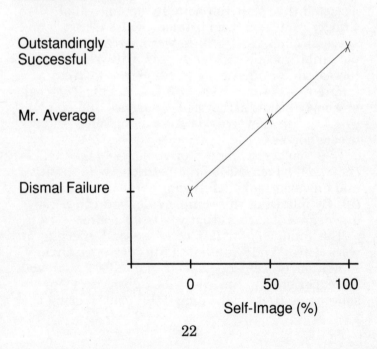

It would be useful to establish, with reasonably accuracy, where you appear on this graph. It is a fair assumption to say that you are considerably *above average*, simply because you are, by reading this book, making a determined effort to improve your chances of success. To evaluate your present position with a little more precision, study the areas I have listed on the following pages then on a scale of 0 to 100 per cent, determine a realistic and honest score. Only you will see these scores, and the more inaccurate your answers, the less effective the test becomes.

Before you begin, look at the graph once more and mark a cross somewhere between 'Dismal failure' and 'Outstandingly successful' according to how you see yourself today. By projecting this horizontally until it intersects with the straight line graph, and then vertically, determine a percentage figure that will represent your self-image.

SCORE...................%

1 LEADERSHIP – The ability to direct success-fully the actions or options of others.

100% ⊤ People always look to you for leadership, whether it be at work, in the gym, in your social club or on a committee etc.

50% ┼ Others respect your advice, and will often ask for your opinion on difficult matters and accept and act on your suggestions.

0% ⊥ Nobody ever listens to your suggestions, nor do they ask for your advice. You never get 'your way' in a group activity.

SCORE...................%

2 EFFICIENCY – Having the competence to perform a particular task effectively.

100% ⊤ You are totally efficient, not a minute of your time is ever wasted.

50% ┼ Your ratio of useful work performed to energy expanded is equal (50:50).

0% ⊥ You are incapable of completing a given task within the designated time.

SCORE...................%

3 PASTIMES – This could be any out of work activity in which you participate. (Competitive sport, chess, cards, photography, painting etc.).

100% — You are a champion and compete at National or International level. Or, your work is widely accepted as being 'the best' and is highly sought after.

50% — At your particular pastime, you are just about average. You can see outstanding ability at the top end of your group and complete incompetence at the other. You believe you come somewhere in the middle of these two extremes.

0% — You are a total failure at every hobby or sport to which you have ever turned your hand.

SCORE...................%

4 SELF-DISCIPLINE – The ability to control your actions, feelings and desires, in an orderly fashion.

100% — You never lose control, even in a heated argument. You act on all of your decisions immediately and with complete conviction.

50% — You abide by some of your decisions, some of the time but occasionally find it impossible to reach a conclusion or steer clear of an argument.

0% — You have a complete lack of control over your own actions. You are continually doing things which you later regret.

SCORE...................%

25

5 INTELLIGENCE (Non-Academic) – We are not talking about education here, but how 'smart' you are. Your natural ability to 'catch on', evaluate a situation for yourself and arrive at the best solution.

100% ─ You never make an error. You can gather the facts together, assimilate and assess them and make a studied conclusion. You have never been 'taken for a ride'.

50% ─ You sometimes make errors of judgement. Solutions to problems do not always present themselves easily. You often see 'the obvious' only when it is pointed out to you. But you do, on occasions, surprise yourself, and others, by assessing a situation correctly. So the ability is there. On balance, though, you are probably no 'smarter' and no 'dumber' than the average person in the street.

0% ─ You feel you need help in improving your intelligence quotient. Others seem so much more able to tackle difficult problems and situations. However, all is not lost; you recognise a deficiency and have the will to improve or you wouldn't have investigated the possibilities of this book.

SCORE..................%

6 CONFIDENCE – Assurance in one's own abilities; possessing self-reliance.

100% —

You have an unwavering belief in your ability to perform a given task, never experiencing a moment's doubt. You can work through to the end of a difficult situation, knowing you have the inner resources to cope.

50% —

You possess a certain degree of confidence, which, under intense situations, tends to be diminished. At such times, you withdraw into the background.

0% —

You have a complete lack of confidence, resulting in your introverted behaviour; you need constant reassurance from relatives and friends.

SCORE...................%

7 CREATIVITY – The ability to originate new ideas.

100% —

Original ideas come easily and quickly, aiding your daily routine at work, on the track or in other leisure-time activities.

50% —

You have occasional ideas which have been successfully implemented.

0% —

You don't ever recall having a creative idea. You are always on the defensive, professing to be 'purely a practical person'.

SCORE...................%

8 ABILITY AT WORK

100% — Your ability at work is unquestioned. You are good at your job, a fact that is recognised and rewarded by the company. You are 'the best' and it is acknowledged by everyone.

50% — You receive the occasional word of praise from colleagues but you also recognise that some tasks are not accomplished easily and, from time to time, have to be repeated. You know there is room for improvement.

0% — You find it difficult to progress at work. You cannot perform any of the required tasks effectively. You are always worried that you will be fired so shrink away from tasks that might show up your inability.

SCORE....................%

9 DECISIVENESS – The ability to determine prompt and specific answers or conclusions.

100% — You always arrive at, what you believe to be, the correct decision without hesitation.

50% — Half of the time you make effective decisions, the other half you are left pondering, not knowing which way to turn.

0% — You cannot make a decision over the simplest of problems. You forever find yourself asking, 'but what would you do?'.

SCORE....................%

10 RELATIONSHIPS – (a) With your family.

100% — Your relationship with every member of the family is perfect. You can soothe tempers, solve problems, forgive thoughtlessness, yet make the offenders see the error of their ways.

50% — There is less friction between your family members than there is between most other families that you know, but things could be better.

0% — You are unable to get along with any member of your family. There is continual stress, bickering and argument.

SCORE.................%

11 RELATIONSHIPS – (b) With friends, acquaintances and colleagues.

100% — You are admired and respected by everyone that you meet. You have an easy-going manner, are a sympathetic listener and give good, practical advice when it is asked for. You make friends easily.

50% — You are reasonably well liked and have just about the same number of friends as most.

0% — You are generally disliked, and have trouble with any prolonged relationships.

SCORE.................%

12 IMAGE – How you feel others see you. (Not how you would like them to see you.)

100% — It is clear that everyone sees you as their equal or even their superior. They aspire to emulate you in every way.

50% — You are seen as a fairly average sort of person, no better and no worse than most people.

0% — You are convinced that everyone looks down on you, and sees you as inferior in every respect. So, when you try to impress someone the right words will not spring to mind and you appear even more stupid. It seems to be a vicious circle.

SCORE....................%

Now return to the beginning of this section and total all twelve scores. Dividing this figure by twelve will give you the mean score as a percentage.

AREA 1 ———%	AREA 7 ————————%
AREA 2 ———%	AREA 8 ————————%
AREA 3 ———%	AREA 9 ————————%
AREA 4 ———%	AREA 10 ————————%
AREA 5 ———%	AREA 11 ————————%
AREA 6 ———%	AREA 12 ————————%
TOTAL ———%	÷ 12 = ————————%

The test will obviously become more and more comprehensive, with the number of zones or areas that are taken into consideration. For our purposes, however, the composite score above will give a fair evaluation of your self-image.

How does this figure compare with your original 'guess'? Do you find that you are actually more successful or less successful than your original figure would indicate?

Well, one thing is for sure, both figures are considerably lower than they should, or could be.

Although it may be hard to believe, the percentage self-image rating resulting from the previous test was largely determined by the time you had reached your sixth birthday. Extensive research in this area has produced overwhelming scientific evidence to support this theory. Furthermore, once a level has been established for your inadequate self-image, circumstances and experiences in the following years will do very little to affect it. In other words, you are stuck with it, and because you are unaware of its existence (or importance) you can take no deliberate steps to alter it.

The direct result of this inbuilt restrainer is that the average man will never surpass 10% of his natural potential. After all, who, at the age of six, is convinced of their own abilities to cope with the everyday hazards and decisions of a 'grown up' life?

The inadequacies that we are now faced with evolved through conditioning in those first few years. By conditioning, I mean the 'do's and dont's', the lessons that we were taught and more importantly the way in which we were taught them.

Consider this example:

As a very little girl, Gemma toddles into the kitchen where her mother is baking some cakes. Intrigued by the whisking, beating and rolling which is going on, she soon begins to emulate the actions of her mother.

31

At this point the conditioning of Gemma's self-image could take one of two directions. Her mother could give her a safe but satisfying task, offering guidance and praising her efforts. This will have a very positive effect on the little girl's self-image. And if the sequence of events is repeated, then confidence will be built through the *habit of success* in this activity.

Conversely, her mother could shun her attempts to join in. Repeated efforts from Gemma are rewarded with irritable rejection and finally banishment from the kitchen, for what her mother sees as deliberate disobedience. This will result in a definite negative effect on her self-image, the lesson being – you must not try to better yourself or be ambitious. The lasting effect on the self-image will be proportional to the severity of the punishment (i.e. raised voice, physical punishment).

When, in later life, Gemma is faced with a similar situation, perhaps cookery lessons at school, then she will draw upon the experiences in her subconscious mind, determining her interest in the subject and subsequent success, or rejection to participate, resulting in failure. It is obviously going to be very convenient to lay the blame for most of our shortcomings at our parents' door. If it is correct that our self-image was determined by the age of six, then surely our parents played a large part in that? Certainly their influence would have been strong, but they were probably only repeating the kind of attitudes *their* parents exhibited towards *them*. Parents also have their own pressures and while they will, to a very large degree, have influenced our self-image unknowingly it would not be fair, or wise, to tackle them at this late date or you could do irreparable harm to their own self-image!

Teachers and one's peers will also have had an effect on the mind of a five or six-year-old. If something particularly traumatic happened to knock our confidence for six, we may forget the incident, but the resulting lack of confidence or self-esteem may be with us for ever if we fail to recognise or tackle it.

In view of this it becomes apparent just how important your inadequate self-image can be in attaining the degree of success you require. Fortunately a technique has been discovered which enables people to re-structure their self-image completely, removing any restrictions and allowing them to exploit their full potential. That technique is the foundation of subconscious reprogramming techniques.

CHAPTER FOUR

DEFINING YOUR GOALS

As we have already mentioned, the detailed definition of one's goals is the single most important factor in actually attaining them. Without clear, well-defined goals, success is impossible.

'I want to be a champion', 'I want to be a star', 'I want to be managing director', are these your goals? No, they are merely ideas, dreams. For our purpose we require something outlined in far greater detail. The analysis of your individual desires can be broken down into three categories:

Short-Term Goals – Things you require right now.

Long-Term Goals – Things you require eventually.

Personal Qualities – Attributes of personality and character, that will enable you to reach and maintain your desired levels of success.

(1) Defining your dreams

The first step in this process of evaluation is to define, briefly, all of your dreams and desires, listing them under the above headings.

Remember these lists are confidential, so put it *all* down. Don't be embarrassed to include *everything* that you truly desire. It is very easy at this stage to let your inadequate self-image govern what you do and don't include in your list. Well, ignore that little voice you hear whispering 'don't be silly, you could never do that'! YOU CAN! Everything and anything is possible using the reprogramming techniques.

SHORT-TERM GOALS

It is equally important to detail short-term goals as it is to define your long-term goals. Knowing where you want to go is essential, but you must also know how you intend to get there.

Imagine, if you will, the window cleaner. He knows that he must clean the windows on the first floor of your house, but he has no means of reaching them.

He could balance on the ground floor window ledge, or try shinning up the drain pipe, but it is unlikely that he will ever succeed. What he needs is a ladder. Now this ladder must have both a platform at the top and rungs in between. Without the rungs, it is clear that his ladder is incomplete and any attempt to reach the platform at the top would be futile.

Just as the window cleaner must surmount each rung before he can reach the top, so must you surmount each short-term goal before moving on.

Using the space provided, list every short-term goal that you might have, whether this be getting involved in more projects at work, winning certain contests or championships, beating certain opponents, becoming involved in certain plays, productions or societies... whatever. You can keep the list brief, using only key words or short sentences.

Your short-term goals might look something like this:

1 Get a better-paid job.
  To achieve this: Take a course in word-processing, book-keeping, selling or something relevant in my own field to allow me to get that better job.
2 Have a more active social life.
  To achieve this: Take an evening class in badminton, drama, creative writing etc. with a view to joining a club or society.
3 Get some qualifications.
  To achieve this: Enrol for an exam subject at evening classes.

Short-term goals:

_____

_____

_____

_____

_____

_____

_____

_____

_____

_____

_____

_____

_____

LONG-TERM GOALS

It is for these reasons that you bought *Direct Your Subconscious and Drive to Success '*. These are the dreams, achievements and degrees of success that you wish to attain. Again I would ask you to ignore your inadequate self-image, and write down everything that you truly desire. You may wish only for an organised lifestyle, to overcome some personal problem or depression, or you may be destined for the board of directors, the silver screen or to be a National, Olympic or World champion, the sky's the limit.

Your long-term goals might be:

1 Rise to the top in my profession.
   To achieve this: (i) Take an advanced qualification over a period of years to gain more expertise. (ii) Read widely in journals, periodicals and books relating to my profession.

2 Win a county tennis championship.
   To achieve this: (i) Arrange for coaching lessons. (ii) Practise for three hours a day.

3 Appear on a TV talent show.
   To achieve this: (i) Join a drama workshop and be prepared for criticism. (ii) Enter as many local talent competitions as possible.

Long-term goals:

_____

_____

_____

_____

_____

_____

_____

_____

_____

_____

_____

_____

_____

_____

PERSONAL QUALITIES

Considering the goals which you have listed above, it will become apparent that the effect of these desires is dependent on your possession and application of certain personal qualities. In order to attain and protect your success, you may feel that you require certain intangible qualities that will result in you gaining the respect and trust of others. These desired attributes of character and personality must also be listed.

As most people have difficulty listing these intangible goals, I have prepared a list which you may find helpful in determining the personality factors that your goals require.

Loyalty	Confidence	Will-Power
Composure	Good Memory	Decisiveness
Concentration	Energy	Sincerity
Relaxation	Creativity	Leadership
Self-Discipline	Self-Respect	Ambition

Efficiency	Organisation	Responsibility
Perseverance	Good Public	Aggressiveness
Honesty	Speaker	Friendliness
Enthusiasm	Energetic	Patience
Maturity	Endurance	Optimism
Ability to	Thoughtfulness	Sympathetic
Communicate	Good Listener	Manner

Before you write out your own list of personal qualities look through the following checklist and tick the boxes so that you can get a true picture of your good points – and bad ones! You will already have completed the questionnaire on pages 18–22 designed to gauge the image you have of yourself. By completing this more detailed questionnaire you should have an even better overall picture of a whole range of attributes.

		YES	NO
1	Loyalty Do you ever speak badly of a close friend to others or divulge confidences?	☐	☐
2	Composure Can you keep calm in a difficult situation without losing your temper or turning bright red?	☐	☐
3	Concentration Do you find you are often saying to associates, 'I'm sorry, could you repeat that. I didn't quite catch your meaning'?	☐	☐

		YES	NO

4 Relaxation
Are you able to empty your mind of mundane worries so that you experience a feeling of total calm?

5 Self-discipline
When you bring work home in the evening, can you easily shut yourself away with it, rather than be tempted to watch a favourite TV programme?

6 Efficiency
Do you work to a routine and pattern, either at home or in business life, so that you can immediately lay your hands on anything you need at any given time?

7 Perseverance
Do you ever say, 'Oh, I can't be bothered with this. I give up.' leaving a job unfinished?

8 Honesty
If you were given too much change in a shop, would you go back and point out the mistake?

9 Enthusiasm YES NO
Are you the one who encourages others to do better things, either at work or in the community, and succeeds in filling them with enthusiasm also? □ □

10 Maturity
Do you ever sulk or 'take umbrage' at a remark rather than think that the person who has upset you is himself immature to have said those things? □ □

11 Ability to communicate
Can you, in the simplest way, easily get your message across to people so that they know at once what you want of them? □ □

12 Confidence
When asked to do something a little out of the ordinary, do you shy away from the challenge saying, 'No, I couldn't possibly do that. I wouldn't have the nerve'? □ □

13 Good memory   YES   NO
    Do you find it easy to
    reproduce facts you have
    seen in magazine or news-
    paper articles weeks or
    even months after you
    have read them?

14 Energy
    Are you often listless,
    especially in the late
    afternoon or early even-
    ing, thinking only of an
    early night?

15 Creativity
    In your social group or
    work situation, are you
    the one who comes up
    with the good ideas that
    are acted upon?

16 Self-respect
    Do you ever run yourself
    down to others, saying
    you are not worth much
    really; or moan about ill-
    health or lack of friends in
    an attempt to gain sym-
    pathy?

17 Organisation
    When you are given the
    task of calling a meeting
    or arranging a trip, does
    everything work smoothly,
    with everyone in full pos-
    session of the details?

18 Good public speaker   YES   NO
    When asked to speak in
    public, are you clear, con-
    cise and amusing, without
    deviating from the subject
    or rambling on in a bum-   ☐   ☐
    bling, hesitant way?

19 Energetic
    Would you rather get up
    and do something active
    than opt for a five-minute   ☐   ☐
    'nap'?

20 Endurance
    Have you the staying
    power to see a job
    through, rather than take
    the easy way out and give   ☐   ☐
    up?

21 Thoughtfulness
    Are you always aware
    when others around you
    are not feeling on top of
    the world so that you can
    help them through diffi-   ☐   ☐
    cult patches.

22 Good listener
    Do people enjoy talking to
    you because they know
    you will listen and give
    them the advice they
    need, rather than jump in
    with stories or problems   ☐   ☐
    of your own?

43

23 Will-power
    When embarking on a
    period of self-denial either
    going on a diet or going
    without something for
    Lent, do you usually give
    up long before the end?

                                    YES   NO

24 Decisiveness
    In situations when every-
    one around you is dither-
    ing about a problem, do
    you find it comparatively
    easy to come to an accept-
    able decision?

25 Sincerity
    Do people trust you be-
    cause they know you will
    always give them a con-
    sidered judgement of any
    situation and will not
    resort to false flattery?

26 Leadership
    Are you the one most
    often chosen as group lea-
    der of a project or chair-
    person of a committee?

27 Ambition
    Do you feel you are work-
    ing towards some future
    goal rather than being
    just stuck in some dead-
    end job?

		YES	NO
28	**Responsibility** Do others say to you, 'Will you take this job on, I know I can trust you to see it gets done properly'?	☐	☐
29	**Aggressiveness** Are you quick to take offence before seeking out the true situation?	☐	☐
30	**Friendliness** Are you one of the first to approach a new colleague or neighbour to see if there is any help or information you can give?	☐	☐
31	**Patience** Having given someone a task, can you wait to see the results instead of bothering them to see how they are getting on?	☐	☐
32	**Optimism** When a work project or home D.I.Y. job is going badly, can you keep colleagues' spirits up by urging that you all tackle it positively?	☐	☐

33 Sympathetic manner   YES   NO
Do you find that you are
often singled out for
advice or to listen to other
people's worries because
they know you will listen
well and help, if possible?   ☐   ☐

It should be obvious from your answers which
qualities you possess but, just to double check, look
at the answers below. The positive attitude always
scores 5 points, so if you scored 165 points you are
an absolute paragon!

1	YES 0	NO 5	18	YES 5	NO 0
2	YES 5	NO 0	19	YES 5	NO 0
3	YES 0	NO 5	20	YES 5	NO 0
4	YES 5	NO 0	21	YES 5	NO 0
5	YES 5	NO 0	22	YES 5	NO 0
6	YES 5	NO 0	23	YES 0	NO 5
7	YES 0	NO 5	24	YES 5	NO 0
8	YES 5	NO 0	25	YES 5	NO 0
9	YES 5	NO 0	26	YES 5	NO 0
10	YES 0	NO 5	27	YES 5	NO 0
11	YES 5	NO 0	28	YES 5	NO 0
12	YES 0	NO 5	29	YES 0	NO 5
13	YES 5	NO 0	30	YES 5	NO 0
14	YES 0	NO 5	31	YES 5	NO 0
15	YES 5	NO 0	32	YES 5	NO 0
16	YES 0	NO 5	33	YES 5	NO 0
17	YES 5	NO 0			

Now list the qualities you possess – be honest –
then you can work towards improving on the grey
areas.

The qualities I possess are:

_____

_____

_____

_____

_____

_____

_____

_____

_____

_____

_____

_____

_____

_____

(2) Reviewing your goals

The second step in goal development is essential, if the lists that you have defined are to be effective. The exact, precise goals developed during this second stage, will form the basis for all of the following work.

The completion of this stage requires you to review each and every one of your goals, from each of the three categories, and modify it in accordance with the format that I have outlined below.

The modified goals must then be recorded with explicit detail, in a separate notebook and kept for reference purposes.

Checklist

Use the following checklist to elaborate on each goal determined in part 1 of this procedure. After applying *every* point of this checklist to *each* specific goal, record the result.

DO NOT PROCRASTINATE! *Act now*.

(a) **Is this something that you truly desire?**
Have you included it because you think that it will impress someone if they should read it?
Have you included it because you know that it is well within your grasp, 'there for the taking' as it were?
Has this been included as a result of a thoughtless comment or caustic remark by a colleague or acquaintance?
These are definitely not the correct reasons for pursuing a goal. If they are your reasons, then discard this goal.
This must be something that you really yearn for.

(b) **Is this goal realistic?**
By realistic I simply mean, is it possible for a human being to achieve. It would be unrealistic to say 'I want to walk on water' or 'fly through the air unaided'. But if this particular goal is attainable by *someone*, then it is

realistic. (At this point in time you may well doubt whether that someone could actually be YOU, but do not worry, this is a result of the inadequate self-image, which we are in the process of correcting.)

(c) **Does this goal contradict any other goal?**
For example, are you saying in one instance that you want to be manager of your department at work within six months, and in another instance that you want to be running your own company, full time, by Christmas? To resolve any such contradiction, choose the higher of the two goals, i.e. The initiation of your own company.

(d) **Have you expressed this goal in positive terms rather than negative terms?**
i.e. 'I want to gain a GCSE in Maths and English in two years' time by attending evening classes.' as opposed to 'If I try taking a GCSE in Maths, I hope I don't fail it again, or, worse, give up half-way through.'
You must express each goal in terms of what you want, not what you want to get rid of.

(e) **Could this goal be any higher?**
Have you set this goal, thinking that any more would sound greedy?
Has the goal been limited because you are concerned about how you would ever attain anything more ambitious?
Is the goal lower than it should be because you cannot *imagine* yourself achieving anything greater?
It is immensely important that you do not limit your goals. By setting your goals only moderately higher than your present level of

achievement, you are not succeeding, and you will never succeed.

Every goal must represent the ultimate achievement, the pinnacle of your desires. Remember, if it is possible for *someone* to attain then it is possible for *you* to attain.

If what you really want is to become World Champion or the highest paid actor (or actress) in Hollywood, then that is what you must write down. Nothing else will do.

(f) **Is this goal specific?**

For example:

Non-specific: I want to run farther than I did last week.

Specific: I want to run for 1 hour each morning before breakfast.

Non-specific: I want to rise higher in the company.

Specific: I want to work as efficiently and consistently as possible so that I can take over when our present Head of Department retires in 18 months' time.

Elaborate on each goal, giving specific details on every important aspect, for this is a plan and without this explicit detail it will be ineffective.

(g) **Does your goal have a deadline?**

Without defining an 'achievement date' for each goal you are effectively prolonging their eventual accomplishment.

Allocate realistic 'achievement dates' to each

of your goals, so putting them into perspective and allowing you to attain each individual goal in a logical fashion

(h) **Is this goal stated in present tense?**
It is crucial that each and every goal be stated as if you had already accomplished it.
i.e. I am a member of the Royal Shakespeare Company performing... etc.
I am competing this year in the National Judo Championships.
I have established my own profitable company making... etc.

The following work is dependent on your goals being stated in this fashion, so it is critical that you ensure every goal complies with this form.

(i) **Does this goal involve the co-operation of family or friends?**
If so, can you guarantee that they will not be against your achieving it. Problems in this area may well prevent you from attaining your goals, so if you feel that it is necessary, talk it over with the person concerned.

(j) **Have you included the important intangible goals or personality factors necessary to cope with the new situations and circumstances that the pursuance of your tangible goals will create?**
I must emphasise the importance of these personality factors in accelerating your progress. Without them, if you manage to succeed at all, the pressures and tensions of your success would become intolerable.

Once you have completed all these lists (short-term goals, long-term goals and personal qualities) in

51

accordance with the above guidelines then you may continue.

COMPLETING YOUR LIST – COMMON GOALS

In addition to the goals that you have now recorded on paper, I would ask that you include the following. They are general goals, the application of which will do much to shorten your road to success. I would advise that you write them in red ink, underline them or highlight them in some other fashion to emphasise their importance.

(i)   With every day that passes, I become more effective, steadily progressing towards my ultimate goal. No situation arises that I cannot overcome with complete confidence and self-assurance. My feelings and subsequent actions are no longer governed by an inadequate self-image, and I am therefore positive and determined, functioning at 100% of my potential.

(ii)   My success is assured and does not require me to take advantage of any other person. I will succeed with or without the help of others and regardless of any temporary set-backs.

(iii)   I strive for excellence in everything that I do, and consistently exceed myself. I always speak the truth and practise fidelity resulting in the trust and friendship of others.

(iv)   If a particular situation or person begins to annoy or irritate me then it is *my* problem. I must, and I do cope with these situations by changing my attitude and/or expectations towards them. As a result of this I enjoy a tolerant and pleasant disposition.

(v) As I proceed with my practice of reprogramming, I am becoming progressively more competent at performing the techniques involved. I therefore accomplish each goal with increasing ease and speed.

You will now have a complete and precise plan for the future describing, in great detail, every ambition, dream or desire that you may have. It is the foundation for all the work to come, so keep it safe.

I would strongly advise that the existence of these plans is kept a closely-guarded secret. Tell only those who are taking the steps with you, as the doubt and scepticism of others may contaminate your own mind, depriving you of the opportunity to succeed. Take no chances.

CHAPTER FIVE

UNDERSTANDING THE MIND

As a simple overview, your mind consists of three parts: The Conscious, The Unconscious, and the Subconscious.

THE CONSCIOUS mind is the logical portion and has the ability to compare, evaluate, determine and the power to reason and be critical.

THE UNCONSCIOUS mind is involuntary and is concerned with self-preservation.

THE SUBCONSCIOUS mind is the most powerful, yet the least understood aspect of the mind. It has no ability to reason, no critical factor and will therefore accept any idea offered to it as truth. If not controlled this energy is wasted on negative emotions or simply left untapped.

Once you are aware of this, it is possible to influence your subconscious to channel energy towards positive goals, towards creating a new self-image, combining the physical attributes and perhaps more importantly the emotional qualities and personality factors that you desire.

This, as you have probably realised, is the principle behind the subconscious reprogramming technique.

In order to understand the procedures of reprogramming and, in particular, a tried and trusted technique that I call HYPNO-SUGGESTION, it is necessary to understand *how* and *why* it works.

Referring to the graph on page 56, you will see a correlation between your level of consciousness and certain activities which we all experience at one time or another.

At the top end of the scale we have *complete consciousness*, a wide awake condition with a certain degree of muscular tension, perhaps with a high secretion of adrenalin. One might experience this condition whilst participating in a fast competitive sport involving speedy reactions and a high degree of concentration. Another situation which might provoke this condition would be one that involved a certain degree of danger, such as motor racing, or downhill skiing. Fear or terror will also cause your level of consciousness to rise sharply to this alert condition.

100% ⊤ (a) *COMPLETE CONSCIOUSNESS* – Both mind and body alert. i.e. during a game of squash, driving a formula one racing car, any situation where there is an element of danger or terror.

(b) *CONSCIOUSNESS* – Awake, but mind pre-occupied. i.e. performing routine tasks at work, driving a car on public roads, reading a book etc.

(c) *BARELY CONSCIOUS* – Vaguely aware of surroundings, i.e. waking up after a long sleep, falling asleep.

(d) *DREAM SLEEP* – Unaware of surroundings but mind still active.

(e) *DEEP SLEEP* – Recovery stage, recuperation.

0% ⊥ (f) *COMA* – Unnatural sleep from which you cannot be awakened.

Moving down the scale, our level of consciousness falls to the normal, comfortable living condition. It is at this level that we perform most of our daily activities such as going to work, driving the car, walking the dog etc. Towards the bottom end of the scale we become increasingly tired and our consciousness slides still further down the graph until we eventually fall asleep. This sleep will consist of both dream sleep and deep sleep. Beyond this, at the very bottom of the scale is *coma*, a relaxation so complete that a person in this state cannot even be aroused medically.

Moving on, it can be determined that our level of acceptance has a direct relationship with our level of consciousness. This is illustrated below.

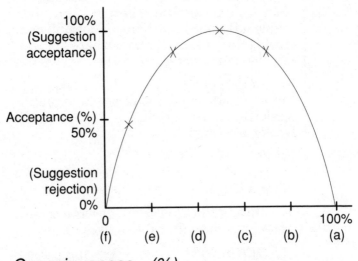

Consciousness (%)

(a) Complete consciousness   (d) Dream sleep
(b) Consciousness   (e) Deep sleep
(c) Barely conscious   (f) Coma

Studying the graph you will see that suggestion rejection occurs at two instances; complete consciousness and coma.

If you will imagine for a moment two tennis stars competing in the finals at Wimbledon. Their concentration is devoted to the game that they are playing, intent on the movements of the ball, and of their opponent. They are, in effect, at the point of *complete consciousness*. In this condition they are completely oblivious to the shouts of the crowd.

If you now imagine the opposite condition, *coma*, where the person experiencing this is impossible to waken, then it can be seen that they too are unaware of their surroundings.

Returning to the graph, the level of acceptance is shown to rise steadily from both of these extremities, to a point somewhere between the two where we reach absolute suggestion acceptance. This occurs at a level of *bare consciousness* when we are only vaguely aware of our surroundings, for instance, as we are waking up from a deep sleep, or as we are falling asleep.

This can be demonstrated by imagining a person awakened in the middle of the night from a sound sleep. If, as they awake, someone were to shout *'Get out of here the room's on fire!'* or *'Run for your life, the house is collapsing!'* they may be fooled into jumping out of bed and making for the door. WHY? Because their conscious mind is not capable of telling them any different, and their subconscious mind, with no powers of reasoning, must therefore accept the statement as truth.

In this suggestion acceptance condition, the level of consciousness is, obviously, far down the scale. Thus it is more readily accessible to suggestion.

If we could devise a simple, but reliable technique that would enable us to induce the exact degree of consciousness required and therefore simulate the *suggestion acceptance condition*, then you must agree, this would be an extremely powerful and useful tool.

If the technique would also allow us to maintain this lowered level of consciousness long enough to implant *positive* ideas or to re-sculpture existing thought patterns in our subconscious mind, then you begin to realise just how immensely powerful this tool could be.

Fortunately this technique has, through extensive scientific research, already been discovered and perfected. It is, of course, what I refer to as the Subconscious Reprogramming Technique.

Hopefully, if you have read this chapter carefully, you will now understand why this technique works, and how we can utilise it to reprogramme our subconscious mind, removing the mental restrictions which have, in the past, prevented us from reaching our full potential. All that remains now is for me to teach you the techniques involved and show you how these may be implemented.

CHAPTER SIX

POSITIVE
REPROGRAMMING

Asking you to re-arrange your subconscious mind and change existing thought patterns sounds a very tall order. Although the human brain is potentially capable of an infinite number of thoughts, analysing complex situations and evaluating billions of different circumstances, we do not use our brains to their full capacity. As I have already mentioned, it has been estimated that we use no more than ten per cent of our total mental faculties, leaving a staggering ninety per cent of the mental potential of a normal human being untapped.

You may well still believe that you are unable to improve on your present degree of success, that you are incapable of exploiting your full potential. This is, without doubt, a falsehood and a result of your inadequate self-image. Before you can progress any further up the ladder to success, you must rid yourself of these negative beliefs in your own inadequacies. The successful people to whom you aspire, do not necessarily possess greater physical or mental powers than you do. Their success is due to the correct application of powers that we all possess, and the belief in their own worthiness and ability to succeed.

To reach any goal or attain something or some level of achievement requires thought, determination, effort and self-discipline. It is much easier, and much more comfortable in the short term, to accept what you have, and this is what the majority of people do, becoming Mr. and Mrs. Average. This, however, is not you. You are obviously prepared to make an effort, and you are doing that at this very moment.

It is important that you understand that you do not have to remain at your present level of success. Don't accept that you aren't as good as the next man, you are. You can achieve *anything* that you really want. Think along these lines and it will prepare your mind for the tasks to come.

Start right *NOW!!* Imagine yourself having reached your goal. Start to plan what you are going to do next, see yourself sitting in the manager's office at work, winning the Mr. Universe contest, receiving the gold medal at the Olympics, or whatever else your personal desire might be. Imagine how you are going to handle the situations that come with your new found success. Or see yourself being interviewed by Terry Wogan on the Wogan Show, think about the kind of questions that you would be asked and how you would answer them.

Don't treat this as an exercise to be carried out whenever you have time. It is a way of thinking that you must adopt ALL of the time. See yourself as a successful person, an achiever. Whilst the people around you are saying 'I can't' or 'it's impossible' you must stand up and say 'It can be done, I can do it', and then show them. Let other people see how positive you are, show them that whatever they can do, you can do better, or bigger, or for longer.

By doing this you will begin to condition your

mind into believing that you can succeed, you can achieve whatever you set out to achieve. Furthermore, by constantly visualising yourself at the point of goal fulfilment, this image will become etched in your mind, strengthening your desire to achieve it, and establishing the belief that anything less than this is unacceptable.

This is more than simply daydreaming or fantasising, it is positive conditioning directed at a specific goal. This conditioning must overflow into every area of your life, thus creating an overall positive attitude, which will, in the course of time, become habit. To determine how much work needs to be done in this area, I would like you to answer the following questions. Answer truthfully: nobody will see the results except you.

The more inaccurate your answers, because you have answered in the way that you think you should, then the less useful this test will become.

The test is laid out in the form of multiple choice answers. All that is required is for you to tick the appropriate box collecting, in this process, a certain number of points.

Before proceeding, enter a figure in the space below, which you feel represents how positive (or negative) your present attitude is.

Choose a figure between 0 and 100.

1 How often do you fantasise about reaching a certain goal, or achieving a certain degree of success?

	Tick	Points
(a) Frequently		10
(b) Occasionally		5
(c) Never		0

2 Imagine that you are due for a rise at work and you are expecting something in the region of 6–8%. When your manager calls you in to discuss it, he offers you only 2.5% do you:

	Tick	Points
(a) Complain bitterly – perhaps taking it to higher authorities?		10
(b) Accept it grudgingly?		5
(c) Accept it without question? (i.e. that must be all you're worth)		0

3 How often do you hear yourself saying 'Oh, I can't be bothered'?

	Tick	Points
(a) Never		10
(b) Occasionally		5
(c) Frequently		0

4   If I told you that you could achieve any degree
of success that you truly desire, if only you are
prepared to change your attitudes, would you:

	Tick	Points
(a) Accept this, believing in your own ability to fulfil it?	☐	10
(b) Doubt that it was true, but be prepared to give it a go?	☐	5
(c) Reject the possibility of any truth in this statement?	☐	0

5   When you had completed your list of goals,
and were comparing each one with the checklist, how many had to be adjusted up because
they were not high enough? (See Chapter 4 –
Item e).

	Tick	Points
(a) None of them	☐	10
(b) Some of them	☐	5
(c) All of them	☐	0

6   How often do you find yourself telling other
people to 'have a go', or to convince them they
are capable of doing something if they will
only make the effort?

	Tick	Points
(a) Frequently	☐	10

(b) Occasionally ☐ 5

(c) Never ☐ 0

7 How often do you find the reverse situation to No. 6 occurring? (i.e. Other people trying to convince you to 'have a go').

	Tick	Points
(a) Never	☐	10
(b) Occasionally	☐	5
(c) Frequently	☐	0

8 How often do you find yourself becoming depressed or frustrated about your inadequacies? (e.g. Does everyone else seem to be better than you? Why can they do it, but you can't?).

	Tick	Points
(a) Never	☐	10
(b) Occasionally	☐	5
(c) Frequently	☐	0

Think of a particularly close friend. How do you see yourself in direct comparison to them?

	Tick	Points
(a) Generally better than them at most things.	☐	10
(b) Just about the same as them.	☐	5

(c) Generally worse than them
at most things. ☐ 0

10 Whatever your own personal goal may be, how effective are you in this area now, compared with six months ago?

	Tick	Points
(a) Unquestionably a lot better than you were six months ago.	☐	10
(b) About the same as you were six months ago.	☐	5
(c) Generally worse than them at most things.	☐	0

Add up the number of points that you have acquired, according to which box you ticked for each answer.

Question No.1	_____ Points	6	_____ Points
2	_____ Points	7	_____ Points
3	_____ Points	8	_____ Points
4	_____ Points	9	_____ Points
5	_____ Points	10	_____ Points
		Total	_____ Points

How does this figure compare with your guess? Did you actually feel that you were more, or less positive than this test would indicate?

Use the second figure, that is, the one obtained as a result of the test, as a guideline to determine how much work you should put in to improve your outlook or attitude. To the extent that your score was below fifty, then you should make a definite and dedicated effort to rectify the situation. To the extent that your score is above fifty, then less work is required.

However one thing is for sure, whatever your score is, it can be improved. To prove this to yourself, and ensure that you make the necessary effort, I would like you to take this test again, exactly one month from today, mark the date in your diary or on your calendar NOW!!

Original guess   _____

Result of 1st test   _____

Result of 2nd test   _____

CHAPTER SEVEN

SUBCONSCIOUS REPROGRAMMING TECHNIQUE

THE STORY SO FAR

In the previous chapters I have taught you everything that I feel you need to know, about yourself, and how reprogramming can re-mould your self-image. If you have followed each chapter, reading and understanding, carrying out each test and performing every task, then you will have a better insight into why you have been unable to attain that elusive success and what can be done to overcome this mental restrainer.

Reviewing the story so far: In chapter one I offered several techniques to enable you to absorb all the information that I was to give you, allowing you to reap the maximum benefit from reprogramming. Then I devoted a whole chapter to the importance of eliminating any scepticism that may have contaminated your mind, preventing you from participating in the important tests, or believing in the ability of reprogramming to fulfil your dreams. Next came the evaluation of your self-image, demonstrating how an inadequate self-image evolves and the lasting effect it can have on an individual's life, preventing them from ever surpassing 10% of their natural potential. A test was laid down to enable you to determine the severity of your own inadequate self-image. Chapter four was dedicated to the importance of goal definition. Having determined a list of goals in each of these three categories, you will have re-written every one in accordance with certain guidelines, preparing them for use with the reprogramming technique. After this I wrote a chapter to explain the fundamental functions of each conscious, unconscious and subconscious portion of the mind or psyche. I went on to demonstrate how we can tap into the subconscious mind at a particular level of consciousness, allowing us to implant positive ideas at a precise point, called suggestion acceptance. Following this we attempted to evaluate your attitude, highlighting any trend towards positive or negative thought patterns and taking the first steps towards correcting your inadequate self-image.

This concludes our story to date. All that remains is for me to teach you the techniques of reprogramming and show you how they may be utilised.

THE TECHNIQUES

There are two basic techniques to be learnt, the first of which is called 'Consistent Image Conditioning' (or Affirmations) and the second which is called 'Hypno-Suggestion' (or Autohypnosis). Both techniques require the use of the goal lists that you prepared earlier, so dig these out and review them. It is not unusual for your goals to alter slightly or change direction, so read through them now, making any necessary modifications.

I would suggest that, from now onwards, you review your goal lists on a regular basis, ensuring that they are a correct representation of your current desires. So start as you mean to go on and do it now!

Are you sure that they are now correct?

Then we'll begin.

Consistent image conditioning

You may well be familiar with the Coué technique for improving self-confidence. Emile Coué believed that anyone lacking confidence should repeat to themselves, several times each day: 'Every day in every way I am getting better and better'. How silly! Well no. This technique, although very simple, is founded on the very same principles as image conditioning. If you are amongst the number who wouldn't recite this, because it obviously isn't true and you don't believe it, then you are suffering from an inadequate self-image. For this reason alone, you are the very person who should be reciting this phrase on a daily basis. It was never intended for the people who truly believe that they are successful, they don't need any help.

So how does this technique work? It relies on impregnation of the subconscious mind with positive ideas, through consistent repetition. If you can recall, the subconscious mind has no powers of evaluation or reasoning and will therefore accept any suggestion offered, as the truth.

Therefore repeating the phrase at a reduced level of consciousness, (nearing suggestion acceptance) will enable you to access the subconscious mind at its most vulnerable. This is the principle on which sleep tapes work. The tapes are intended to alter your thought patterns by simply playing them at night, within earshot, whilst you are sleeping (perhaps this is a technique you could incorporate in your own improvement programme.

Remember the page number, refer to it if and when you feel it necessary).

Image conditioning is a refined version of the Coué technique, operating under the very same principles, but in a far more precise and individual manner. Imagine how effective it would be, if you could use your pre-defined goal lists, taking each goal, tangible or intangible, and using it in place of Emile Coué's phrase 'Every day in every way', etc. etc. And, instead of simply repeating this throughout the day, if you deliberately recited these goals at a point when your subconscious was at its lowest. ...

That's it – Consistent Image Conditioning.

This is the format that your conditioning should follow:

1. EACH MORNING

(a) Keep your goal lists within arm's reach of the bed. (I am referring to the goals prepared in accordance with the checklist, that is, those written in a positive, accomplished form, not the short form lists prepared earlier.) As you awaken each morning, as soon as the alarm sounds (i.e. don't press 'slumber'!) sit up, reach for your lists and proceed to read every one, aloud if possible. I would suggest that you set your alarm for half an hour earlier than normal. This will disrupt your inbuilt time clock, ensuring your drowsiness, and will prevent you from rushing your declarations.

(b) After reading each goal, concentrate on the 'key words' or phrases, visualising the fulfil- ment of each. Do not rush this process; take your time. Enjoy the feeling of satisfaction, see the reaction of others, bask in the glory of success. Let yourself be 'carried away' totally enthralled in this new satisfying image.

Only when you feel totally at ease and comfortable with this picture of success, should you move on to the next goal. As I have already mentioned, do not be too hasty, let it take as long as necessary.

2. EACH EVENING

As you sit in bed at night, no matter how late it is or how tired you are, repeat the morning process. Do not deliberately retire early, so that you can complete this process before you become too tired. If anything, retire slightly later than usual. Having made the decision to go to bed, undress, clean your teeth etc. then sit quietly in an armchair, relaxing, for about fifteen minutes. Get into bed and perform your conditioning routine until you can no longer keep your eyes from closing. If at any point during the night you should awake, feeling thirsty, the need to relieve yourself or for any other reason, then this is another perfect opportunity to repeat your affirmations. Make good use of it.

It is absolutely essential that your conditioning routine be carried out, as I have indicated, on a daily basis. Do not skip a session because you feel 'too tired', in this case more is definitely better, and the more time and energy you devote to your practice of the reprogramming techniques the quicker you will begin to reap the benefits. If you are not prepared to practise regularly the application of these techniques, then you will considerably reduce their effectiveness; only consistent practice pays off.

71

I would advise that you become familiar with the technique of image conditioning before progressing. Re-read the method that I have outlined, and if you feel that it will be useful, write it out on a separate piece of paper, or better still in the same book that you recorded your goal lists. Begin your first session tonight; there is no reason whatsoever to delay.

To help you to remember your image conditioning sessions, I have drawn up a form that you can remove and pin on the wall next to your bed. Simply place a tick in the appropriate box after each morning and evening session.

Hypno-suggestion

By now, if you have followed my advice, you will be practised in the technique of consistent image conditioning and therefore in far better position to tackle the next step. Hypno-suggestion, when used in conjunction with your affirmations sessions, will ensure the most rapid results possible. Although very similar in nature to the use of image conditioning, it is a great deal more powerful and therefore capable of accelerating your progress.

As with image conditioning, hypno-suggestion is designed to operate at that level of consciousness when the conscious mind and subconscious mind are capable of communication. Whereas previously we have made use of the two instances in a normal day (i.e. first thing in the morning and last thing at night) when we naturally pass through this point, with hypno-suggestion we actually induce and maintain this condition for as long as is necessary. Because your awareness is linking the conscious and subconscious regions of the mind, you are able to relay instructions and suggestions from the former to the latter.

Although this technique is often referred to as 'autohypnosis' or self-hypnosis there is nothing to fear. It is not possible to become locked in a state of trance, unable to awaken yourself. The condition you will experience is similar to that of a light sleep with full conscious awareness. With practice you will find that you are able to reach a far lower level of consciousness thus improving the effectiveness of this technique. If however you go too deep, then you will simply fall asleep and wake up naturally.

PREPARATION

Unlike image conditioning, which allows you to work on every goal each session, hypno-suggestion may only be used on one goal at a time. Once you have chosen a goal from your lists, you must continue to use only that one for hypno-suggestion, until you have attained it. For this reason you should choose whichever you feel to be the most important quality first and then work down in descending order. Take out your goal lists now and arrange them in order, writing the most important at the top of the list. Obviously this new list must be written in a logical order, short-term goals first, then long-term goals.

For example, for the dedicated and ambitious weight-lifter the list might look like this:

List 1

Goals (Tangible)
- (1) I can clean and jerk 150lb
- (3) I am the club champion
- (3) I can deadlift 500lb
- (4)
- . (Goals steadily increase until...)

.
.
.
.

(10)   I am the National Weight-lifting Champion
of Great Britain

.   (Even higher goals are set)

.
.

(15)   I am a Gold Medal winner at the 1996
Olympics

Now prepare a second list for all of your intangible
goals, again placing the most important of these at
the top of the list.

For example:

List 2

Goals (intangible)

(1)   I possess an abundant supply of energy and
draw upon it at will.

(2)   I can bring great concentration to bear on
any subject at any time.

(3)   I possess great confidence in my own
abilities in any situation.

(4)

.   (Continue to write the goals in descending
order of importance)

.
.

(10)   I am able to relax deeply at any time.

For the best results I would suggest that you select
goals alternately from each list. Tangible goal the
first day, intangible the next and so on. As you
attain each goal, cross it off your list, select the
next one and proceed.

74

Once you have chosen your first goal, select two or three key words and commit them to memory. This is necessary as hypno-suggestion is performed with the eyes closed, and attempting to memorise the entire declaration would be tedious. You may find it useful to highlight these key words on your goal lists with red ink or by underlining.

You will require both the goal written out in the long form and your chosen key words for the practice of hypno-suggestion, so ensure that these are prepared before each session.

FORMAT

Hypno-suggestion should be used only when you are reasonably alert. Do not use it first thing in the morning, last thing at night or just after a heavy meal. If possible set aside a particular time of day (e.g. having washed or showered after returning home from work, but *before* the evening meal) and then repeat the process of hypno-suggestion once a day, every day, at this designated time. The entire procedure will take the following steps:

(1) Prepare the first goal on your list.

(2) Go into a quiet, dimly-lit room and sit down in a comfortable chair. Relax for five or ten minutes.

(3) Read the full declaration slowly and carefully, visualising and concentrating as you would for image conditioning.

(4) Pick out the key words from your declaration and repeat them to yourself, out loud if possible, once again visualising the picture of success.

(5) Follow the method that I have outlined in the

following pages, to reduce your level of consciousness to a semi-hypnotic state.

(6) Repeat the key words from your declaration *silently* to yourself, allowing them to re-create your mental picture of the successful fulfilment of this goal. Spend as long as you want in this condition. Enjoy the feeling of success and accomplishment. See, in your mind's eye, how easy it was to attain this goal and therefore realise your hidden potential. Remain in this light trance long enough for your subconscious mind to absorb completely the positive suggestions that it is receiving.

(7) Return to full consciousness. As you rise slowly from this semi-hypnotic state, repeat the following phrase to yourself:
'I feel more ENERGETIC, more ALERT, and better DISCIPLINED than I have ever felt before'.

You will have to memorise this phrase, or the key words or simply the principle, to enable you to benefit from it when you are, once again, fully conscious.

That's all there is to it. Hypno-suggestion is a very simple technique to learn and a very enjoyable one to practise. Do not, however, get carried away under the false belief that more is better. Unlike image conditioning, where repeating your affirmations several times a day is beneficial, hypno-suggestion must be used only ONCE a day, and on only ONE goal at a time. You will find that your goals are reached a lot sooner than you may think, allowing you to progress steadily down your goal list. How quickly can you expect to attain your goals? Well, it is entirely dependent upon you and the frequency and consistency with which you perform both image conditioning and hypno-suggestion.

METHOD

Hypno-suggestion entails removing outside awareness of the body and the mind to enable selective conditioning of the subconscious.

Initially it may be a strange sensation, but through consistent practice you will be able to relax completely and eliminate tension in no more than 30 seconds. However, if you consciously resist, you will be unable to enjoy the short and long term benefits of this technique. You *must* accept this conditioning process completely. If you have belief and desire, the success that you are seeking is, without doubt, attainable.

Before outlining the procedures involved, there are two common faults which will hinder your progress, unless avoided. Firstly, you must not force it to happen, let it happen, it is a gradual process that you must allow yourself to become accustomed to. As I have already mentioned, it will, with regular use, become almost second nature. Secondly, do not attempt to analyse or evaluate what is happening; this will prevent you from reaching complete relaxation and make concentration impossible.

The technique has been broken down into six simple stages. Read and re-read each step until you are confident that you understand how to perform each one without having to refer back to this book. Every time that your hypno-suggestion is interrupted, you must start again from the very beginning, so it pays to ensure that you understand each individual stage, and in which order they are to be performed.

First stage

Go into a quiet room where you will not be disturbed. Close the door and any open windows, and take the phone off the hook. Sit down in a comfortable chair and relax. Reduce your rate of breathing by pausing on each breath, after you have exhaled and before you inhale. Spend five or ten minutes on this process (longer if you feel that it is necessary). Once you are sure that you are totally relaxed and calm, take out your chosen goal, which you will have already prepared for this session. Read through the entire declaration, concentrating on every word and its meaning. Now close your eyes, visualise this goal at the point of fulfilment, imagine every detail and experience the feeling of achievement and pride flow through your body. Repeat to yourself the key words from your declaration, thus associating them with this picture of success. Once you feel that you are ready then continue to the next stage.

Second stage

If you are totally relaxed and comfortable in your chair, then remain there for the whole session. If you would rather lie down on your back, on a bed or on the floor, then do so, (use a pillow or some other means of support for the head if it will make you more comfortable). Extend your arms slightly to the side of your body, palms down and separate your legs. The idea is to have no two parts of your body touching, so there is no need for extreme or uncomfortable positions. (It is beneficial to wear loose-fitting clothing in which you feel comfortable: top buttons, ties and spray on trousers are definitely out. I would suggest that you remove any jewellery that you may be wearing.)

Third stage

Focus your gaze on a spot on the ceiling, directly above you. Concentrate only on this spot. Now, begin to draw in long deep breaths through your nostrils and exhale gently through your mouth, feel yourself begin to 'let go'. Pause between each breath. Each time that you exhale you should feel your body relax further and further, your muscles will loosen and your eyelids begin to grow tired. Let them close.

Fourth stage

The next stage is called fractional relaxation, and involves relaxing successive parts of your body. With practice it is possible to develop total loss of body awareness and it is at this point that the subconscious mind is open to communication and vulnerable to suggestion.

With your eyes now closed, concentrate all of your attention on your feet. From the toes to the balls of your feet, down the arch, all the way to the heel. Imagine your feet turning to lead or stone, feel them become increasingly heavy. (Remember you must fully accept what is happening, and feel comfortable with the procedure.) Now let this heavy feeling flow into your calves and slowly up your legs to your thighs. With each breath, as you exhale, concentrate on your legs, feel them grow heavier. Feel this wave of relaxation creep upward into the groin and buttocks. Slowly it flows up through your abdomen to your solar plexus. Feel yourself slipping deeper and deeper into a heavy slumber. Now relax the lower back fully and feel this relaxed heaviness flow up the spinal cord and enter the muscles of the back. Feel it flow over your shoulders and into your chest. Now feel it flow down both arms, all the way to the fingertips,

79

causing your hands to become heavy. Now this deep relaxation and heaviness flows gently back up your arms into your neck and throat. Feel it flow up the back of your head, relaxing every muscle and nerve as it goes, onto your scalp and then flowing down over your forehead into the eyes. Concentrate on your eyelids, they are so deeply relaxed that you find it difficult to open them. You should now be experiencing some loss of body awareness, your mind will be tranquil and your subconscious receptive to your positive suggestions.

Although it sounds very simple, when correctly executed it will produce an extremely pleasant and enjoyable feeling, like nothing that you have ever experienced before. To reach this lower level of consciousness you must remain intent, your concentration focused at all times throughout the process. Every body part must be subjected to this intense relaxation, the process *cannot* and therefore *should not* be rushed.

Fifth stage

Repeat the key words of your declaration to yourself, visualising as you do the satisfactory accomplishment of this goal. Hold this image in your mind for as long as possible, see the reaction of those around you and the expression on their faces. Step, temporarily, outside your body and watch yourself, see how confident you are and how easily you cope with the situation. It becomes obvious that you are, without a doubt, the very best. Now move back inside your body, feel the success, feel the pride surge through your body, that wonderful feeling of accomplishment. Remain in this condition until you are totally comfortable with the situation and your subconscious mind saturated with images of success.

80

Sixth stage

When you are ready to return to full awareness imagine that you are standing at the bottom of five steps and that when you reach the top you will be fully aware, refreshed, relaxed and eager to meet the demands of the day. See yourself slowly climbing the steps. When you reach the top step, open your eyes, take a deep breath and stretch.

As I suggested earlier you may wish to repeat the following phrase, as you climb up each step:

'I feel more ENERGETIC, more ALERT and better DISCIPLINED than I have ever felt before'.

The entire process should take fifteen to twenty-five minutes. In the beginning your mind may drift in and out of awareness, but remember, this is a totally new experience and like any discipline, you may expect to master it only with persistent practice, enthusiasm and belief.

Memorise the process, have someone read it to you as you go through it, or, using a cassette recorder, prepare a tape that you can replay during your session, whichever you find easiest.

If you intend to prepare your own cassette tape, then I would advise that you cover the first, second, third and fourth stages only, i.e. those which convey you from awareness to lowered consciousness. Stage five should be performed in total silence, any external noise would only serve to distract you.

As you employ the hypno-suggestion technique, you will gradually develop more and more control over the way that you think, feel, act, and react. Continued practice is essential to develop proficiency in both image conditioning and hypno-suggestion. In using the methods that I have described you will experience increased self-control that can be applied to all aspects of your life.

With this increased control, you will realise your ability to effect beneficial changes, and eventually facilitate the attainment of every one of your goals.

The effective use of the subconscious reprogramming technique

How do you know if you are effectively using this technique in your day-to-day programme? With consistent image conditioning you can only assume that if you are following the instructions every day, at least twice a day, then you will receive the maximum benefit.

And similarly for hypno-suggestion, if you are following every stage, including correct preparation, once every day then you should accelerate your progress. But how do you know that you are reaching the required level of consciousness for the effective use of hypno-suggestion?

This is extremely difficult to define for it is a highly personal or subjective feeling which, when achieved, is evidence of the correct state.

This does not mean that there exists a certain level of consciousness, below which hypno-suggestion is effective and above which it is not. The procedure that I have described will work at any point along the spectrum, the effect being proportionate to the degree of consciousness that you reach. 'Practice makes perfect' and the more consistently you practise both image conditioning and hypno-suggestion the better you will become, the quicker you will be able to descend to lowered consciousness, and the more effective the technique will be. But remember, do not try too hard, you cannot speed up the process by rushing. Take my word that if you practise regularly you will be able to reach a deeper level of consciousness, with greater speed and less effort.

SUMMARY

To help you in your practice of both consistent image conditioning and hypno-suggestion, I have noted below a concise guide to both techniques, listing the major points.

Consistent image conditioning

(i) Use this technique at least twice every day and always first thing in the morning and last thing at night.

(ii) Read your declaration aloud if possible.

(iii) Read every one of your goals at each session.

(iv) Do not rush.

(v) Complete Table 1 (p. 85) on a daily basis.

Hypno-suggestion

(i) Use this technique only once a day every day.

(ii) Select one tangible goal (as in List 1, p. 73) and one intangible goal (as in List 2, p. 74) and use hypno-suggestion on these goals only, until they have been attained.

(iii) Select key words from each goal and memorise them.

(iv) Use hypno-suggestion only when you are reasonably alert.

(v) Do not force yourself to reach lowered consciousness.

(vi) Do not attempt to analyse or evaluate what is happening.

(vii) Complete Table 2 (p. 87) on a daily basis.

As for consistent image conditioning, I have prepared a table that you may use to keep track of your daily sessions. I would suggest that you remove it from this book and fix it to the wall, next to Table 1, by the side of your bed.

Simply fill in the months at the top of each column and place a tick in the relevant box, after each session. I have prepared each table for a five-month period. However, you need only continue filling these in until your image conditioning and hypno-suggestion sessions have become habit.

TABLE ONE: CONSISTENT IMAGE CONDITIONING

Month										
Day	a.m.	p.m.	a.m.	p.m.	a.m.	p.m.	a.m.	p.m.	a.m.	p.m.
01									.	
02										
03										
04										
05										
06										
07										
08										
09										
10										
11										
12										
13										
14										
15										
16										
17										
18										
19										
20										
21										
22										
23										
24										
25										
26										
27										
28										
29										
30										
31										

TABLE TWO: HYPNO-SUGGESTION

Month					
Day					
01					
02					
03					
04					
05					
06					
07					
08					
09					
10					
11					
12					
13					
14					
15					
16					
17					
18					
19					
20					
21					
22					
23					
24					
25					
26					
27					
28					
29					
30					
31					

CHAPTER EIGHT

UTILISING YOUR UNCONSCIOUS MIND

I have shown you how to use your subconscious mind for attaining your goals; now let me show you how to utilise your unconscious mind to complement these procedures. To realise the potential of the unconscious mind, let us study an element of Freudian theory.

FREUDIAN THEORY

Sigmund Freud (1856–1939) described the human mind as consisting of two main regions, comparable to an iceberg. The tip of the iceberg, projecting above the surface of the ocean, represented the conscious region of the mind, the unconscious region was represented by the invisible mass below the surface of the water. To the conscious region, he assigned the thoughts and feelings of awareness, accessible only during the waking state of consciousness. To the unconscious region he assigned the records of experience, feelings and sensations of every occurrence in our lives up to the present day, including those that occurred during early infancy. This is illustrated on the following page and clearly demonstrates the massive untapped potential of the human mind.

This figure also shows how the unconscious mind can access information gathered from past experiences, apply them to a present situation and then transfer the correct answer, suggestion or decision back into the conscious region of the mind. This invisible portion of the mind is rarely, if ever, utilised by the average person: the day they learn how to use it, they cease to be average. For you, at least, that day has arrived. The final step in your programme for success requires the ability consciously to access the unconscious mind.

FREUDIAN THEORY
THE MENTAL ICEBERG

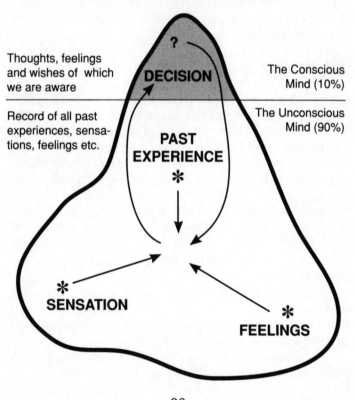

The fulfilment of your goals relies on the ability of your unconscious mind to devise a successful method for attaining them. The solution or answers offered by your unconscious mind must then be successfully transferred to the conscious region, enabling you to receive or become aware of them.

It is possible that you already benefit from the use of your unconscious mind, unknowingly. If you have ever had a 'hunch' that solved a problem for you, been unable to think of a name although it was on the 'tip of your tongue' and then remembered it later on that day, or when faced with an important decision you decide to 'sleep on it', and awaken the next day with the answer, then you have been putting your unconscious mind to work.

You must, however, develop this power to the extent that you are able *consciously* to assign your unconscious mind to a particular problem. Once again, the technique is extremely simple and for this reason is often rejected. Don't limit yourself in this manner: try it and you will find out for yourself.

The unconscious mind may be applied to goal achievement in two different ways. The first is *Problem Solving* and the second *Recuperation*. The perfection of these techniques will accelerate your progress in the area of goal fulfilment, by eliminating any problems that stand to obstruct your route to success.

1 Problem Solving

A problem is no more than a difficult decision, the burden of which increases in direct ratio to the complexity of the problem. If the situation is either yes or no, do or don't, black or white etc. then the arrival at a decision is usually less difficult than if there are numerous solutions, from which you must choose the best course of action. In the latter case it is easy to see how the problem can grow out of proportion, causing us to worry, perhaps lose sleep, and end up making a hasty and often incorrect decision. This behaviour is obviously non-productive and will almost certainly slow down your programme of goal fulfilment. When we are faced with a complex problem, presenting us with a lot of information of varying degrees of importance, a number of answers of varying worth and emotional pressures, why struggle with the ten per cent power of our conscious mind when we have the ninety per cent power of the unconscious mind at our disposal?

To reassure you of the ability of the unconscious mind and its problem-solving capacity, let us look at the decisions in a process as simple as scratching an itch. First there is the awareness of the itch. Then, the decision: to rub with the back of the hand? To rub with the fingers? To scratch with the nails? How many fingers? Which hand to use? How long? How hard must you scratch? Is there an article of clothing in the way? Should it be removed? Or lifted? Or dropped? Is the selected hand free to scratch or must some burden be put down first? Where shall you put it? etc. etc. These are merely the highlights of a number of decisions that can enter into a simple act, and which will all be solved in a split second.

In addition to acknowledging the need to scratch, innumerable calculations must be made in order to carry out that decision effectively: i.e. How far to lift the hand? How far to bend over, flexing and unflexing the chosen fingers, positioning those fingers on the exact point on your body where the itch occurred, perhaps out of sight behind your back?... and so on, and so on.

Such a simple activity, carried out by an average human being, requires that decisions and computations be made which are so numerous and which require such a complex input of information from different sources in such a short period of time, that no computer in existence today could handle it.

Now think of a slightly more taxing situation which again we take for granted, such as driving your car home from work in the rush hour traffic. A computer programmer's nightmare! Imagine having to write a programme that could assimilate all of the information relating to speed and proximity of other vehicles, the side of the road, the middle of the road, judging distance, noting the little boy playing with his football, traffic lights, dogs, mind reading (will the car pull out on me?). The decisions and instantaneous calculations which have to be made are immense, yet we take them for granted. This is because we do not have to make the conscious decisions or perform the calculations; they are all carried out unconsciously.

In view of this, you must agree that any problems that you are faced with in your conscious mind would be insignificant and easily solved if turned over to the unconscious mind. Well, that is exactly what we intend to do.

There are four clearly defined stages in this process, which, if used correctly, will stimulate the unconscious mind, allowing the problem which exists in the conscious mind to pass through into it. Once your unconscious has the problem, you can forget all about it, the answer will come back to you in due course. Does this sound a little bit too simple? It is, but it works!! TRY IT.

METHOD
(1) Once you have realised that you have a problem which cannot be easily solved, write it down on paper. Sit down and work the whole thing through in your mind, then carefully and accurately state the problem, clearly defining it from start to finish. This alone will go a long way to easing the burden, for I have found that many problems exist only because of the muddled, confused arrangement of thoughts and information relating to the decision. Once you are happy that you have outlined the problem clearly and precisely, write down all of the possible solutions. State briefly how each solution could solve your problem.

(2) You will now understand the problem completely and be aware of all its possible solutions. Consciously try to answer it yourself. Take another piece of paper and draw a line down the centre. At the top of one column write 'PROS' and at the top of the other write 'CONS'.

Now take each one of your possible solutions, one at a time, and write down all the reasons for taking this decision in the 'PROS' column and all the reasons against taking the decision in the 'CONS' column.

It is possible that, during this procedure, you will find that you are able to make the correct decision, thus solving the problem. Spend long enough, trying to solve it consciously, giving yourself time to come up with a solution. Once you are convinced that you cannot solve the problem, proceed to step 3.

(3) This is the most difficult step to accept. Try to imagine your unconscious mind as a computer: you have defined the problem and presented all of its possible solutions with the reasons for and against each one. The computer now has all the information that it requires to enable it to solve the problem. All that remains is for you to type in 'RUN' and press 'ENTER'. That's it! Simply ask your unconscious mind to commence with the process of problem solving. If you are dubious that a problem of such magnitude could be solved by simply asking your unconscious mind to take care of it, let me refer you to the example of driving a car. (A far more complex problem than anything that is likely to occur to your conscious mind.) How often, when driving to work in the morning, have you suddenly become aware that you must turn off the motorway or road which you are on? You have become so involved with your conscious thoughts, that coming back to reality is almost like being awoken from a sleep. Not only this, but you are unable to recall clearly the specifics of your journey. You have been driving on 'automatic pilot' letting your unconscious mind do all the work whilst you 'daydream'. Your actions are more than force of habit, for conditions on the road are never the same two days on the run.

If these procedures are followed, then I can assure you that the unconscious mind will deliver the goods. Accept that, and your unconscious will work for you, too.

In addition to asking your unconscious mind simply to solve the problem, you must also specify when you require the solution. Repeat to yourself 'I need the answer to this problem by tomorrow morning', or '... by six o'clock this evening', or '...

by next Saturday'. Be realistic when issuing a deadline, don't delay a decision which must be made and conversely don't try to rush the process. The complexity of a problem will influence how quickly a solution will be found, so give your unconscious as long as possible.

To start the process working, you must forget all about the problem. The conscious and unconscious minds will not work on the same problem simultaneously, so dismiss it, secure in the knowledge that your unconscious will solve it. Continuing to worry will only hinder you now, delaying the eventual realisation of the solution.

As with the techniques of reprogramming, proficiency will come with consistent use. However, if you properly prepare your problem as I have outlined, your unconscious mind will respond. If you consciously believe that it won't work, then you will prevent its functioning. You must *accept* that it does work, *believe* in the immense power of your unconscious mind (remember Sigmund Freud's mental iceberg) and you will be rewarded with the benefits of its use. Considering the tremendous advantage of consciously being able to apply your unconscious mind to a specific problem, the decision to accept that it will work for you, should not be a difficult one to make.

(4) The final step is knowing how to accept the solution from your unconscious mind. There is nothing mystical or mysterious in this, the solution will simply 'come to you' as you are walking down the road, driving the car, washing the dishes or performing any other task that does not require deep concentration. Whilst your mind is otherwise preoccupied, it is not receptive to any thoughts from your unconscious, therefore you should expect

to receive the solution to your problem during a period when you are relaxed, and not thinking about any one thing in particular. The answer will 'feel' right, it will seem so obvious that you will probably wonder why you were unable to solve the problem immediately.

The realisation of that solution, however, is not always obvious. A particular phrase from a song or book, something that you were once told, an individual's face etc. are all possible means of conveying the solution to your conscious mind. Whichever way that it arrives, directly or indirectly, you will find that it repeatedly appears in your thoughts until you recognise it as the solution to your problem. Generally, the answer will come to you in a direct form, immediately recognisable and ready for application to your problem.

Do not fail to act on this decision without delay. If you leave it for a few days, or a week, or fail to act at all, then it may be some time before your unconscious will function properly again. You cannot escape or hide from your unconscious, it is with you at all times and knows every action and decision that you make.

INSTANTANEOUS SOLUTIONS

There is a technique for nearly instant application of your unconscious mind. If a particular problem requires an almost immediate decision, then you should proceed as follows:

(1) Prepare your problem as outlined in steps 1 and 2 of this chapter.

(2) Select key words from each solution and

repeat them to yourself, allowing them to recreate the complete solution.

(3) Use the method detailed in chapter 7 for hypno-suggestion, reducing yourself to a lowered level of consciousness.

(4) Repeat the key words of each solution, visualising each one and its subsequent results as you do so.

(5) Ask your unconscious to solve the problem. Tell yourself that you need a precise answer to this problem – immediately.

(6) Empty your mind, and simply exist in this relaxed state, enjoying the sensations of lowered consciousness until a solution emerges. This should only take a matter of minutes if your preparation was thorough.

Again, I would point out that you cannot fool your unconscious mind into rushing a decision. Therefore the instantaneous solution technique should only be used when a problem actually requires an immediate answer. If you are consciously aware that there is no urgency, then you are also unconsciously aware and the above technique will be of no use.

Why is all this business of problems and problem solving important in goal fulfilment? Because to be successful you must first be effective and efficient. Neither of these essential personality factors is attainable if the mind is choked up with a confusion of unsolved problems. This will inevitably result in restlessness and anxiety, which are definitely not the traits of a successful person. To be successful it is necessary to have a clear mind, free to tackle current situations and make important decisions.

Possessing the ability to be able to access consciously the immense power of your unconscious mind, which remains inaccessible to most people, is surely an asset and one which should be used as frequently as required in your programme of goal fulfilment.

As you will recall, I mentioned that there were two ways in which we could apply the powers of our unconscious mind to the quest for success. The first of these being *Problem Solving* and the second *Recuperation*. Let us now have a closer look at this second application.

2 Recuperation

Research has shown that although the number of hours sleep required varies between individuals and also with age, the belief that only four or five hours are needed is fallacious. Actual requirements conform more closely to the practice of sleeping seven, eight or nine hours a day as is commonly accepted.

Assuming that your requirement for sleep is actually eight hours a day, then approximately the first four hours are devoted to bodily repairs, or the rejuvenation of tissues which have been worn down or damaged during the previous day.

In observing this period, scientists noted that during the first hour, sleep is particularly deep, with an accompanying increase in basal metabolism and an extra expenditure of energy, involved in the elimination of physical fatigue. The remaining hours' sleep is somewhat lighter, requiring considerably less energy. During this period the more intricate repairs are carried out – such as reflexes and various physically derived judgements such as distance, form, colour etc. This is accomplished through cell repair and reproduction.

99

During this second phase of light sleep your unconscious works (primarily through the use of dreams) to lower the tensions and pressures which have accumulated during the day. If you have been subjected to intense pressures and stress throughout the day, you will require more sleep to recuperate successfully and completely. If this is not possible, or you just didn't get enough sleep during the night, your mental rehabilitation will be incomplete upon awakening.

We have all experienced the results of this, for example: irritability, lowered tolerance, reduction in your nervous and mental capacities and so on. Problems can grow out of proportion, increasing tension and, once again, pressure. This is obviously extremely destructive and will, if allowed to continue, severely impede your progress.

It is at such a point as this, that you should utilise the following technique, permitting your unconscious mind to complete the process of mental recuperation.

METHOD

(1) Make a conscious decision that the time has come for a recuperation session.

(2) Find a quiet room (if you are at work, you may wish to go outside and sit in the car) and sit, or lie in a comfortable position. Loosen any restrictive articles of clothing e.g. undo your belt and the top button of your shirt. If possible, remove your shoes.

(3) Slowly reduce your rate of breathing.

(4) Close your eyes and relax. Tilt your head back slightly, relieving any tension in the muscles of your neck.

(5) Feel a gentle wave of relaxation flow slowly through your body, from your feet to the top of your head.

(6) Don't deliberately try to empty your mind. Focus on the blackness directly in front of you (the back of your eyelids). Now begin to imagine that darkness seeping in through your eyes, slowly filling your head.

(7) Remain in this relaxed condition until you feel an uncontrollable desire to open your eyes... do so. Inhale deeply and stand up.

The entire process should take between five and twenty minutes to perform, and will leave you feeling refreshed, enthusiastic and full of energy.

Again, if this technique is used on a daily basis, its effectiveness will increase, and the time required to perform it will be reduced.

WARNING!!
On completion of your recuperation session, you may find that you wish to close your eyes again and continue this pleasant experience. DO NOT!!

As soon as your eyes are open, inhale deeply, pause, exhale then stand up and continue with whatever it was that you were doing prior to your session. A second treatment, directly after the first will probably leave you feeling dizzy and result in a headache. So, for the best results, adhere to the one session a day rule.

This technique will not only aid your mental recuperation, but will also increase the ability and speed with which you are able to access your unconscious mind (thus enhancing the success of the problem solving function). To help you get into the habit of setting aside time for daily recuperation sessions I have prepared a table for your completion. As with Tables 1 (consistent image conditioning) and 2 (hypno-suggestion), Table 3 should be removed from this book, and fixed to the wall by your bed, serving as a reminder and record of your daily sessions.

Simply fill in the appropriate months at the head of each column and then place a tick in the relevant box after each session.

TABLE THREE: RECUPERATION

Month					
Day					
01					
02					
03					
04					
05					
06					
07					
08					
09					
10					
11					
12					
13					
14					
15					
16					
17					
18					
19					
20					
21					
22					
23					
24					
25					
26					
27					
28					
29					
30					
31					

CHAPTER NINE

STRESS RELIEF

Do you ever suffer from headaches, indigestion, sexual problems, high blood pressure, infertility, asthma, or insomnia? Any of these disorders may indicate an overabundance of stress or an inappropriate reaction to it. It is quite safe to say that every human being alive today is subject to some form of stress. The day-to-day demands of living present us all with some sort of stress, against which the body and mind take the necessary steps to defend themselves. This usually results in an increased secretion of stress hormones (adrenalin, cortisone). These hormones allow us to perform in an increased capacity, therefore improving our ability to cope with a particular stressful situation. Stress is simply a reaction of the body and mind to the demands that they are faced with. In moderate forms it can be a definite aid in assisting the body through pressured times. However, left unchecked, stress can have extremely tiring and destructive effects on an individual. When a stressful situation occurs, the body must adapt to the subsequent increase in the level of stress hormones. If these stressful situations continue to occur over a sustained period of time, the body's reaction may become habit. This could result in an extreme reaction to otherwise unimportant situations, with the mind developing a tendency to exaggerate the problem. Eventually, this will take its toll, leaving the person involved feeling tired and listless.

The causes of stress are not always as obvious as they may seem. In addition to the 'shock' and 'fright' situations, of which we are aware, there are also everyday routines producing continuous stresses which often go unnoticed. This could be working at a job which you dislike, with a set of people with whom you have nothing in common, or getting caught in a traffic jam when you are late for an appointment, or coping with unemployment or even being left alone with young children for long periods of time. In effect any situation which results in a feeling of tension or frustration will produce stress. Let us now define two common reactions that have a direct relationship to stress.

The first of these is 'worry'. If you worry, you are very well aware of what is troubling you. It is a response within your conscious mind to a situation or circumstance about which you are concerned.

Anxiety, the second of these reactions, is a profound feeling of worry for which there is no foundation or good reason. This is because the cause of anxiety is generated within the subconscious mind and therefore inaccessible to the conscious region of the mind. For this reason, no appropriate conscious action may be taken to relieve the feeling of anxiety.

Both of these reactions, (worry and anxiety) may be considerably reduced or eliminated by the use of hypno-suggestion. For this technique, as we have already discussed, will allow us to reduce our level of consciousness to such a point where a direct link is created between the conscious and subconscious portions of the mind. Through hypno-suggestion and the deep mental, emotional and physical relaxation developed with its use, accumulated tensions can be discharged and the capacity to endure stress enlarged.

This technique is an extension of the procedure that I outlined in the previous chapter to aid recuperation. Whereas for the purpose of recuperation, we rely on simple relaxation and clearing of the mind, for stress-relief we must reduce our level of consciousness to such a point where we can access the subconscious mind. In achieving this and creating a sense of peacefulness and serenity we are able to bring an exaggerated problem or situation back into perspective, thus alleviating any feeling of anxiety.

The method that you should use is as follows.

METHOD

(1) Prepare for hypno-suggestion exactly as outlined in chapter 7.

(2) Slowly reduce yourself to the lowered level of consciousness, as you have previously learned.

(3) Once this receptive condition has been reached, let your attention focus on your breathing. As you exhale each breath think of the words 'down' and 'relax' enabling you to slide gently into a deeper tranquil state. Continue this for approximately fifteen to twenty breaths until you feel calm and untroubled.

(4) Now concentrate on emptying your mind. Look into the blackness directly in front of you, (your eyes will be closed by this stage) and imagine it seeping in through your eyes, slowly filling your entire head, and saturating your mind.

(5) Simply exist in this state for as long as it feels comfortable.

(6) Now, out of the darkness, begin to visualise a tranquil scene in your mind's eye. This could be anything, any environment in which you feel totally peaceful and comfortable, perhaps an open field, a forest, a deserted beach, a mountain-side or rolling hills.

(7) As this picture becomes clear, let all of your senses become totally absorbed in the peace and beauty of your relaxing environment. Feel the warmth of the sunshine, the gentle breeze on your face, hear the waves lapping on the beach or the grass whispering in the wind. Become totally engrossed in this scene, calm and free from any problems.

(8) Remain in this condition for approximately fifteen minutes before returning to full awareness as described in the method of hypno-suggestion (p. 77).

I would suggest that you practise this technique for stress relief no more than once a day, and at least once every two days, depending on your own daily requirements. In doing this you will find that you can actually prevent the undesirable reactions to stress from occurring. This is a far more efficient way of coping with stress, rather than waiting until you have been affected, then applying this technique as a cure. (Although it will work effectively in both situations.) As I have already mentioned on numerous occasions, proficiency is the result of regular practice. This is very important as, to gain the maximum benefit from any one of the techniques that I have offered, it is essential that you become skilled in the application of each one.

Once again, to keep track of your daily sessions for stress relief, I have prepared a table for your completion. If you feel that you are slowly beginning to re-paper your bedroom wall with these tables, how about filing them in a binder or folder and keeping this on your bedside chair or table? The whole object is to remind you every morning and every evening of the tasks which you must perform, so don't bury them under a pile of magazines in a cupboard or drawer. Within six months, you will have become so accustomed to these routines that they will be performed through force of habit, thus removing the need for the continuing use of these tables.

TABLE FOUR: STRESS RELIEF

Month					
Day					
01					
02					
03					
04					
05					
06					
07					
08					
09					
10					
11					
12					
13					
14					
15					
16					
17					
18					
19					
20					
21					
22					
23					
24					
25					
26					
27					
28					
29					
30					
31					

CHAPTER TEN

THE ELIMINATION OF FEAR

The emotion of fear is probably the greatest inhibitor of positive action and plays an overwhelmingly important role in the conditioning of the young child. As it is this early conditioning which is responsible for the formation of our inadequate self-image, the resultant fear can be a tremendous detriment to our consistent improvement and success.

Frequently we experience our energies working against us instead of for us, as we try to work around accepted limitations and barriers rather than trying to eliminate them. In the past, through incorrect application and utilisation of our energy, we have been unable to develop our true potential. As a result of this we find that we cannot act and react in the way that we truly want. Although fear is very specific and personal in nature, the following generalisations may be made.

(i) The unconscious mind is primarily concerned with survival. Based on information, feelings and experiences gathered throughout your life and stored in the unconscious element of your mind, certain reactions have been developed for a given stimulus. Should a fear-evoking stimulus occur, the response will be one of self-preservation. The fear to which I refer is not the fear of failure or criticism.

113

but the fear of how to cope with that failure or criticism.

(ii) Fear stems from an unknown entity: it is a fear of some future possibility, not of a current situation. If you have no comparative experience upon which to draw, you will feel insecure and look for assurance.

(iii) We are capable of attaining a certain degree of success, regardless of our inhibitions, as we can usually find ways to overcome these fears (but not eliminate them). However, if left unresolved, these fears can develop into anxiety. The first negative effect of anxiety is an increase in blood pressure. Prolonged periods of anxiety will result in a form of adrenal failure (a restriction in the release of the stress hormone adrenalin), making even the most insignificant problems seem like a heavy burden.

To demonstrate how easily the young mind can be filled with negative and destructive thoughts, let us look at a few phrases often unwisely meted out as a form of punishment.

'You will never learn anything.'
'You are so stupid.'
'You never do anything right.'
'Why are you so clumsy.'
'You will never be as clever as your brother/sister.'
'You will never be any good at that.'

When we add to this the unintentional conditionings brought about by accidents or childhood mistakes (for example, breaking objects and doing or saying the wrong things) then we can begin to appreciate how our inadequacies and fears of failure were created. If these lessons were only present in the conscious mind they would be easily forgotten and have no effect on our later life. Unfortunately, the more severe the punishment and the harsher the word that is spoken, then the more firmly etched the lesson will become in the subconscious mind. And as the subconscious mind has no powers of reasoning, no critical element, they are accepted as truth. This can be illustrated by considering dreams that we have had in the past, in which impossibilities seemed quite reasonable to our subconscious minds, ('I was talking to my wife when she became a grotesque monster'... 'I was floating through the air'... 'the room vanished and I was standing in a cave'.) Whilst we are asleep, any one of these circumstances would be accepted without question. To the conscious mind however, they are immediately recognised as impossibilities.

So we have established that, as well as fears that currently exist in our minds, we have also got certain inbuilt fears lodged in our subconscious mind as a result of conditioning during our early childhood.

The limiting effect of fear on our performance may be greatly reduced by utilising reprogramming techniques and, in particular, hypno-suggestion. Through the consistent use of this technique we can incorporate positive, confident and success-oriented suggestions into the subconscious mind. If you have a strong desire to understand, improve or remove a negative force, then success will eventually be realised.

It is easy to be weak and allow fear to maintain its grip on you. Desire to change for the better requires strength – strength to admit that you are affected by a fear and strength to overcome it.

The procedure is very similar to that used for goal fulfilment and requires that you detail, very clearly and accurately, every fear which you feel will restrict your progress. As it is often difficult to recognise a restrictive fear, I have listed a few examples to demonstrate exactly what it is we are looking for.

Fear of:

   ... an awkward customer with whom you must deal, preventing you from successfully closing a contract.

   ... an overpowering superior at work, resulting in your inability to communicate and create a good impression.

   ... a particular rival or opponent in the gym, on the track, on the field etc., thus securing the belief that you are second best and therefore giving them an advantage.

   ... flying, heights, water, closed spaces, open spaces, crowded rooms etc. preventing you from attaining one of your goals.

   ... your inability to cope with success. (You don't want to win the trophy for sportsman of the year, because you are too scared to get up and receive it. You would 'freeze'.)

   ... your inability to cope with criticism. (You cannot progress with your acting, modelling, bodybuilding, singing career as you're afraid of what others are saying behind your back.)

Now it is your turn. List every possible fear that you feel is hindering your progress and therefore preventing your success. Don't worry that they will sound 'silly', no one else is going to see them.

116

Often, the mere fact of facing up to a fear is an aid to conquering it.

FEARS:

_____

_____

_____

_____

_____

_____

_____

_____

_____

_____

_____

_____

_____

_____

_____

Once you are sure that you have detailed every one of your fears, rewrite them in order of importance, placing the one single most important fear at the top of your list and the least important fear at the bottom.

At the same time express each fear in a positive form i.e. prefix with 'I am not afraid of... ' or 'I am better than... ' or end with '... does not bother me'.

Do this NOW.

DECLARATIONS:

_____

_____

_____

_____

_____

_____

_____

_____

_____

_____

_____

_____

_____

_____

_____

We have now prepared each fear, presenting it in a form suitable for hypno-suggestion. Choose the first fear on your list and from your declaration pick out the key words. Highlight these using a red pen for underlining or encircling, or by some other means. You are now ready for hypno-suggestion.

METHOD

(1) Find a quiet room, sit or lie in a comfortable position. Ensure that you are isolated from any external interference (telephone, dog etc.).

(2) Repeat the entire declaration, concentrating on the key words. Then repeat the key words, allowing them to re-create a picture in your mind's eye, showing the point at which you overcome this fear.

(3) Proceed to induce a level of lowered consciousness as detailed in chapter 7, on pages 78–82.

(4) Once you have reached this deeply relaxed condition, repeat the key words of your declaration, visualising as you do, a situation in which you are confronted with this fear. Feel the uneasiness and tension that the situation creates.

(5) Now begin to see and feel increasing confidence to the point where you are unaffected by the feared situation or person. Enjoy the feeling of satisfaction and accomplishment that begins to grow inside you. Remain in this position until you feel comfortable, assured of your ability to handle the situation effectively.

(6) Return to full awareness as described on page 81 for hypno-suggestion.

It may take several sessions to eliminate a fear totally, but persistence will eventually pay off.

A word of warning. This technique should be used on just one fear at a time. Progress down your list only when you are sure that you have overcome each fear, and you are totally confident in your ability to cope successfully with any situation in which it may present itself. By advancing too quickly you will probably diminish the effect of any progress that you might have made, and will certainly make no further improvements.

Your persistence and desire to improve will determine the speed and effectiveness of your results. Consistent use of this application of the reprogramming techniques will soon see you addressing and conquering the last fear on your list. Remember, you are truly responsible for yourself and your actions. By progressively eliminating your fears and initiating a more productive way of thinking, you will eventually become the master of your own destiny.

And yes, you guessed it, yet another table to complete (the last one, I promise). Table 5 is designed for use over a five-month period, but surely you don't have that many fears. Use it for as long as necessary.

TABLE FIVE: ELIMINATION OF FEAR

Month				
Day				
01				
02				
03				
04				
05				
06				
07				
08				
09				
10				
11				
12				
13				
14				
15				
16				
17				
18				
19				
20				
21				
22				
23				
24				
25				
26				
27				
28				
29				
30				
31				

ORGANISATION AND SELF-IMPROVEMENT

In the previous chapters I have set down several tables for your use. By completing these on a daily basis, you will be making a dedicated and consistent effort towards the attainment of your goals. It is only through the systematic approach and performance of the subconscious reprogramming technique that your success will be realised. Before six months has expired, you will be competent in the use of these techniques, and the daily routine that is essential to your continuing success will have become habit and as much a part of your routine as eating or sleeping.

Your entire programme for self-improvement is founded upon organisation, dedication and a methodical approach. By following these rules you will accelerate your progress and ensure your eventual success. You are in control of your life. Your position in society today and the degree of success that you have attained reflects how well or how badly you have managed so far. But no matter where you appear on the success scale, you can improve, you can succeed or you can fail: the choice is yours. As soon as you come to terms with this fact and realise that you are truly the cause of all your effects, then you are well on your way to achieving those things that once seemed out of reach.

If you add to this belief, belief in the power of the reprogramming technique, belief in yourself and your ability to succeed and desire to win, then the formula is complete. All that remains is consistent practice of those techniques. Unfortunately most people fail to recognise, or admit to the responsibility that they hold and the controlling effect this has on their lives. It is so much easier to blame other people, circumstances or events, that they reject the truth. We know that reprogramming relies on consistently repeating positive phrases and suggestions until they have become accepted by the unconscious mind.

In the very same way, by constantly repeating timid, negative phrases such as, 'I can't'... 'I can't do any thing about it'... 'It wasn't my fault'... 'I couldn't do that', you will find that these, too, will become implanted and accepted by your subconscious.

The truth is that you are responsible for your actions, and if you have belief and desire then you can change for the better. It is no use saying to yourself, 'O.K. I don't believe in this but I will give it a go', and then setting absurd goals which are impossible to reach, making a half-hearted attempt at reprogramming and then saying, 'See, I tried it and it doesn't work, the whole thing is a farce'. In doing this you are condemning yourself to a life full of failures and non-achievement. You must have belief and desire, for I assure you that if you possess these and you channel them into the dedicated practice of reprogramming then you will succeed.

You should believe that you are capable of achieving any goal that you set, however far away it may seem at present. If you tell yourself this and think in these positive terms, then you will eventually come to accept it.

In this world in which we live, nothing is free, everything desirable has some price attached to it. This could be money, but it is more likely to be time, energy or discipline. You may find, during the pursuit of a particular goal, that you can no longer afford to spend the increasing amount of time that its attainment requires. You may also find that to progress up the ladder, you must move to another part of the country or even another part of the world. Here is a case when you should write out the 'pros' and 'cons' of the situation to give your unconscious mind enough information to help you arrive at a decision. You may consider that the price of success isn't worth the end result, and only you can make that decision. But if you are willing to pay the price, then you can succeed.

Many people will use this as an excuse, an easy way out. When they 'give up' because they can't be bothered any more, they can say, 'Yes, well I could do it as well, but I haven't got the time', or 'I had to pack it in because I am always so tired when I get in from work'. These people will never amount to anything and if you use these phrases in the future you will know you are being less than honest with yourself; if you have the desire you can do anything.

The fulfilment of any goal requires hard work, dedication and 'will-power'. If you are prepared for this and can give it everything that you've got, you should succeed, and that's fantastic. If when you are halfway there, you realise that there is some valid reason that prevents you from continuing (the price is too high), then that's O.K.: you haven't 'failed', but have made a conscious decision not to proceed. But you must NEVER simply 'give up' or 'cop out'.

Think of it in these terms. Subconscious reprogramming is the vessel which could carry you swiftly to the land where all of your dreams will come true. To get there, however, you must row, long and hard. The more effort that you put in, the faster you will get there. There is no doubt in the ability of the vessel to convey you to the other side; the deciding factor is YOU!